I0435759

In the Name of Justice

In the Name of Justice

Garry Johnson

Copyright © 2015 by Garry Johnson.

Library of Congress Control Number:		2015908932
ISBN:	Hardcover	978-1-5035-7539-4
	Softcover	978-1-5035-7538-7
	eBook	978-1-5035-7537-0

All rights reserved. No part of this book may be reproduced or transmitted in any form or by any means, electronic or mechanical, including photocopying, recording, or by any information storage and retrieval system, without permission in writing from the copyright owner.

Any people depicted in stock imagery provided by Thinkstock are models, and such images are being used for illustrative purposes only.
Certain stock imagery © Thinkstock.

Print information available on the last page.

Rev. date: 06/04/2015

To order additional copies of this book, contact:
Xlibris
1-888-795-4274
www.Xlibris.com
Orders@Xlibris.com
712439

DEDICATION

To my Parents and Grandparents who struggled but provided our family with Opportunity and Love.

To my children and grandchildren who I pray benefit from the efforts to provide them a better tomorrow.

Finally, for history, to provide a broader picture of what life was like today.

*T*HERE WAS A *time when there was love.*
      It came before time began when conditions could change and remain unknown.
   It came with a warm glowing emanating from within.
   It was given fuel when held close and tenderly cuddled.
   It put words to shame.
   There was a time when it reigned as the only occupation of life.
   To love and be loved are honorable and spiritually enriching goals for human attainment.
   In appreciation of its gift it serves as payment.
   Love.

   Life is so precarious and dangerous.
   Hate has spurred some on to their greatest triumphs but love was what they wanted to remember.
   Everyone wants LOVE but not everyone will get it.

   Tommy agonized about it daily.

   Living alone was okay. He enjoyed running his days and nights.
   It had been six month's since Eloise left to visit their daughter in California. She never returned and Tommy had decided not to look back.
   He was in control.
   There were some things which stood out.
   He had to recognize his age and the state of his mind and body.

The thirty years he had worked in the Streets department of Philadelphia. He worked out of the Water department and he operated a jackhammer. His legs and arms sometimes felt like jelly and he had fractured bones and stressed ligaments in his foot.

He took medication which kept his troublesome ailments under control but he had to be alert of his condition.

He had to learn moderation. It was a spiritual undertaking.

In these modern times, as society changes we have changed the expectations of just about everyone.

The elderly, due to medical procedures, breakthroughs and physical fitness are living longer.

They say sixty is the new forty.

It all depends on the individuals frame of mind and factors which are beyond their control.

Regardless, the elderly still want to enjoy life as capable, mobile individuals with an appetite for activities which challenge one's concept of age.

Some go to skydiving and mountain climbing while others choose painting and forming a band. Even the coach potatoes are trying to eat healthier. Neither Sex nor Dancing have to be given up.

Nowadays the public streets and transportation as well as the merchants stores have been friendly to the electrical carts which propel those who can't walk.

Tommy still has aches and pains but he wants to live outside of his house and he wants to be in LOVE.

The reality is that as much fun as there is in new explorations, the probabilities for misery is also high.

Social Baggage is a typical inheritance of age.

As the world changes everyday, more and more nuances are positioning themselves to being issues in the future.

Relationships are difficult.

For different reasons men and women find themselves at odds.

The equal status in the workplace negates many of the ancient concepts which governed married life.

The kind of women that Tommy met wanted security and to be pampered. These women wanted all the authority and money that their mates could accumulate. In an era where woman hold all forms of jobs with varied responsibilities, many want to hold men to standards in the fifties. In the same instance, women want to exercise the freedoms and authorities won in the nineties.

The man is still expected to hold the door and pay for the meal of a woman who may be more than capable of providing for herself or them together.

These women love was their love for themselves. They wanted 'sugar daddies' or paying customers.

Poor previous relationships often hurt emerging new relationships.

Tommy had been out to the bars and some special events at neighborhood gentlemen clubs.

In the bars, women always talked about marrying him. When he would mention that his wife was gone someone else would volunteer for the position. If he didn't mention he was married some women would accuse him of some old bull crap and then they would say that if he divorced his wife they would replace her.

Tommy was not interested.

In different areas of the city you can find bars which serve as private club for neighborhood events.

Generally Tommy went to the clubs which featured the music of his youth and had patrons around his same age.

These clubs offered live music and some of the most attractive women of the city. There were plenty of 'Ballers' with two or three tables. There were fashions and designs on style being projected.

The purple or peach men's dress suit, with thigh length jacket and wide legged pants was a mainstay. There were coordinating hats, shirts, shoes and socks. These clubs offered swagger and territorial conquest.

The women Tommy met here were looking for money and fame and they were prepared to take down anyone to get it.

Old dudes, young babes was the demographic here.

At the root of all good relationships is Peace.

Everyone desires peaceful coexistence with the one they love.

The problem, as Tommy sees it, lies with the term LOVE.

As a senior citizen he could see the relevancy of a song sung by the "Spinners", "Its takes a fool to learn that Love don't Love Nobody".

In this world many people fall in love with others but the emotion remains a singular one. Love is often usurped by one, defined by one and controlled by one.

Love truly loves no one but itself.

It can defy reason. Half of the women that Tommy met were their own problems. Good men, men who are good people, are turned away by these women everyday. Men who play the game that they say, they despise are the ones they covet.

Those are relationships which are full of drama and pain.

Tommy is a seeker of peace

In Tommy's world the women thought that meant piece, meaning that whatever men say, all they want is SEX.

It was not that these women were subserviently or peacefully having sex with their men. Despite their remarks they use it like gold.

It was really meant to portray men as liars.

Men have been known to stay with women and never have sex Regardless, men still are seen as liars because next they are staying to be fed and cared for but never are they staying for love.

The men who stay in these relationships, for love, are seen as incompetent and unsatisfactory males.

Men, throughout history, have been cruel to woman.

The history books and police logs are full of domestic abuse and even murder. Before the eighteen hundreds, Men could get away with beating, abusing and even eliminating their wife or their children. The economic structure lend itself in favoring men. Employment and societal mores were narrower and options were seen as blasphemy.

Nowadays that things are changing, everything is Topsy-turvy.

People, from a societal view, are not sympathetic with each other.

There exist a rivalry and competitive environment. In love and capitalism, love can opt for more security. Individual feelings are subject to ridicule and cajoling.

GARRY JOHNSON

The modern day dating environment is a battlefield.

Everyone must stake a claim or make the statement which defines them or their desires.

Everyone harbors some precursor which is used as a template for their relationship and generally it is all about mistakes in previous arrangements.

Eloise's absence gave Tommy the opportunity to experiment.

Tommy had been experiencing it all, within reason.

Being married, living alone and searching for a companion offered many opportunities for Tommy.

Seven month's ago he had gone to Atlantic city.

He had gone with a friend from the neighborhood.

They had a grand time drinking and drugging.

The women were plentiful because it was a 'Players' weekend.

Tommy and his buddy Gene arrived with two ladies.

It was Sex and Drugs every hour. There were four meals and there was music.

Unfortunately, a meeting with two deranged party goers in Atlantic city got Tommy in jail, bruised and sore while Gene, his buddy was beaten by the police. Fortunately Tommy was able to help in the rescue of a kidnapped and abused woman.

He didn't want to duplicate that again.

Since that time he has been more reserved when he ventured out.

Everyday there were opportunities but he didn't take advantage of every opportunity.

Tommy Wilson is the neighborhood philosopher.

He likes to talk but rarely does and when he does, he does so constantly. He had his local and favorite bars to visit.

Tommy could always use some local haunt to hook up with friends and fellow retired employees.

He has closed many of the old hangouts. Many of the crowd that he had commiserated with during those days had died.

Ever since his retirement he has tried to marginalize his trips.

He did not want any driving under the influence charges, he knew that traveling could be dangerous.

Everyday between the chores and watching everything on television, Tommy sat thinking. Here he was sixty three years old and everything was different.

As a young single buck he would who have been out every night, living his life, sampling the world of its many delights.

As an old man he was in, most of the time, alone and thinking.

He was not bringing women back to his home. He never met anyone who could even casually drop by. Even old women steal.

Whatever they don't move or break, they critique. No matter, he didn't want prying eyes and gossipy lips.

Love, the magical concept of Nirvana between two, giving and caring is a hard place to get to when the ocean is full of sharks and whales while the world above the seas are plagued by toxic gases, windstorms and electrical discharges.

People are scurrying to survive.

Tommy was trying to live to the max and everyday he was confronted by these realities.

*T*HOUGHTS ARE LIKE *the rest of life, they become repetitious. The routine of ones day has its normality. You wake up and move around.*

The bathroom, the refrigerator, the television, even the radio and the internet have all been first choices.

We are governed by our desires or responsibilities. Most people work out their necessities to provide for themselves.

Tommy found himself going through the motions as the weeks of the year grew fewer.

He was outwardly talking to himself. He walked from room to room, either talking to the television, singing to the music or answering the queries in his brain.

He was alone. His friends list was saturated by good associates.

Those were the people who he had come to trust to a certain level. These were people who he had forged an understanding.

The people who he had grown up among or near had generally died, disappeared or moved on.

There were still some of the old gang living in the neighborhoods.

Many had moved outside the city.

Eloise was a bridge. He often hated that he knew this.

It was a reality which he rather be free of.

She, even in their world of few words, put him in constant contact with the past. The past was a place he knew, it was a place where he found purpose, enlightenment and love.

Tommy settled back into the comfortable armchair in the living room.

The television was on and a movie he had seen just days ago was on again. He was paying it little to no attention.
For the moment his mind was focused on his wandering thoughts.
He looked at the images and pictures around the room with a blank stare.

The telephone rang for a solid minute.
Tommy sat in his chair talking to himself.

He jumped up, "Wow", he said.
He rushed across the room and picked up the receiver.

"Whatz the fuck is up, Negro"!!!

Just those phrases and then the voice. Who else could it be?
Eugene Watts.

Years ago Tommie had been good friends with Gene's brother, Charles.
Charles died several years ago. Tommie and Eugene formed a friendship based on those youthful days when Charles was still alive.
As they have both grown older the almost four years difference in age is not the problem it was when they were younger.

Gene was a frantic and hyped person.
He came across as a salesman. He flattered the women and pumped fists with the men. He consumes tremendous amounts of liquor and drugs while he attempts to live the good life.
Gene worked as a banking officer and was retiring soon.
He had spent most of his money in leading his amorous life.
He had four children from three different woman and he never saw any of them; he just did enough to stay out of court.

Tommy even found Gene to be crude and disgusting at times.

"Still choking that chicken over there? You got to come with me to a couple places I know."

GARRY JOHNSON

Tommy could hear Gene snorted hard. Knowing Gene he imagined him snorting coke, talking on the telephone, driving a car and caressing an exposed nipple of the female in his company, all at once.

"What's up with you, replied Tommy. I imagine you are flying right now. I guess you just looked down and saw you were over Philadelphia and decided to call."

Gene made the sound of a frustrated horse,
"Nothing so mobile. I am home.
I have been taking days off. I will be retiring soon and I have been checking out some other opportunities."
Gene snorted loudly again.

Gene talked for near to two hours.
Tommy could tell that there was something, some reason why Gene had called.
The two spoke maybe once or twice a month and this seemed unexpected.

In retirement there is a tremendous amount of time for contemplation.
Even the most carefree and bohemian of us all become serious and committed during those senior years.

Gene had become distant to the world as he got older. He vowed to never hurt again after the early death's of his brother and his parents who died before he graduated college.

Gene bounced from one bed to another and danced in the Penthouse parties.
The years when he was a young banker had changed.
He was more reserved and complacent now, which only meant that he had finally grownup.
Gene had talked so much that Tommy knew he should have lost his job several years ago. Instead of going to jail Gene was winding down and cognizant that he would have to change.
He talked about his children's mothers and his children.
He had regrets and explanations.

Tommy had never thought that the trip the two men took to Atlantic City was as big a deal for Gene as it was for him.

Truth be known, it was.

He could hear the air coming out of Gene's balloon of confidence and bravado.

Even through the constant use of profanity and his loud delivery of attitude, Tommy could hear the gradual softening of one bad ass.

The conversation, which was basically one way, interested Tommy.

He had his own thoughts which were driving him insane.

He could emphatically use this to quiet his own mind.

There was not much he could say to Gene. He was beyond help.

Gene was still committed to living hard and fast, combinations which kill old men.

If he actually vocalized all his regrets that would be one full sad year of twenty four hours, three hundred sixty five days of misery.

Since Gene was only slowing down and not stopping it is possible that a year would not be enough.

Somewhere along the line Gene started talking about his remaining living uncle.

Gene's uncle lived in St. Louis, Illinois.

Gene's uncle was his mother's brother. He had worked for the Illinois department of corrections for thirty seven years.

He had no family or children. According to Gene, Uncle Charles (who his brother was named after), had helped Gene financially to finish college after his parents passed on.

Gene described his uncle as a straight arrow. The service within the department of corrections had made him super righteous.

It became apparent ten years after his uncle had retired that his health was going to require that he receive special attention.

Uncle Charles had fought the advice to live in a retirement community. He continued to live alone until a fire which started in his kitchen convinced him that he needed help.

Tommy's mind was still addressing something Gene had said earlier about his former women.

Tommy was agreeing how deceptive and two faced woman could be. He was thinking about how Eloise had treated him.

He had made every effort to make her happy and she ignored him completely.

She said that she loved me, Tommy thought and he blurted out, "but she lied"!

"Who lied"?? Gene asked
Tommy caught himself and redirected the conversation.
"Now what did you say"? asked Tommy.

"I was saying that I could use your help next week. I have to go to my uncle's and pick up some possessions, one of which is a car. You know Man, it's a fourteen fifteen hour drive and we could hang out."

Now Tommy tries to repeat Gene's words by retracing the sounds he had heard.

The whole story of Gene's uncle came back to him.

Tommy had always tried to develop his concentration. He had dabbled in meditation and control. In some, Tommy was seen as an old sage. It was one of the qualities Eloise found too pompous to respect.

Regardless, it was something that Tommy honestly tried to hone. He tried to be a straight arrow and to use what he knew as a benefit to others.

This was an area that he was not too good at….. treating himself.
Gene had become a cautionary tale in Tommy's life.
He would never deny him their friendship but a journey like the one Gene was discussing would entail too many hours together.

He could tell that Gene really wanted him to accompany him on the journey.

Tommy could hear some anguish and panic in Gene's voice.

It sounded as if his uncle was really in a bad way and Gene was afraid/ too emotional to go alone.

He could take a plane, bus or train and get there and have all the time to pamper and indulge in whatever he wanted.

Tommy still had sketchy memories of all the vices he participated in on their last adventure and the memories that were clear advised him not to repeat.

Tommy talked about having two cars to drive back and Gene suggested that they take the train on his dime.

"it will do you good to get out of that house and mix it up a little, said Gene. It's time to live, Man"!

Gene continued to talk about how the trip would be fun but Tommy was stuck on his advice to live.

He needed to get up off the potty, in his marriage, and Live.

Too long had he sat in the house surrounded by his loneliness while searching the meanings of life and love.

The country was changing and all the people here represented an opportunity for him to expand his life.

He had read books and magazines.

Television programs flickered before his eyes while his mind soared to other planes in other dimensions.

He was never going to resolve his condition by lounging around the house or cruising the city hotspots.

He needed a walkabout. He needed to confront his realities.

"Sure", replied Tommy.

In the midst of his wandering mind he had decided.

He would drive across the country and see his wife and daughter.

If he was going to start a new chapter in his life, he would have to leave his familiar surroundings.

He would drive Gene to his destination and then he would travel alone the remainder of his journey. He needed time to think and he would use the scenic value of a cross country trip to sharpen his focus.

"Uh Wait, said Gene, Are you sure"?

Tommy didn't realize that he was speaking his thoughts and plans out loud.

Gene reiterated that he would pay for them to get to St Louis. He even implied that he would go to California with Tommy after he saw his Uncle.

Tommy knew that wouldn't work.

"You know that might be interesting, said Tommy, but this is a journey I have to take alone."

"That's a long trip, replied Gene, we can alternate driving."

"Gene, I don't know what to expect when I get there. I last spoke to them a week ago.
Tommy paused to think, then he continued.
I will drive you to St Louis. I'll stay for a day while you deal with your uncle."

"Yeah, Man, shouted Gene into the phone. We can hangout a little."

"When you're ready to come back home, I will continue my trip out west." Tommy wanted Gene to understand that he planned to travel alone.

W*ITHIN THE WEEK the media was involved in Ferguson, Missouri.*

The Injustice of the American Justice system is as legendary as slavery. The system is set against people of color and poor people.
Caucasian males, aged 10yrs to adult, have killed on College campuses and in loaded movie theaters, and ...., a Caucasian can walk around carrying, openly, a loaded weapon. It has been documented that discussions will be opened between the police and the individual in an effort to ascertain their reasons for being armed and to establish the identity of the armed individual.

In the other communities, being openly armed will get you fired on by police. There would be very little conversation about identity. In these communities the police use their weapons and their abusive, insulting, intimidating authority as communication.
In these communities there have been cases of Police entering the wrong home and killing an innocent. Homeowners, in these communities, can be imprisoned for firing a weapon in defense of life or protection of property.

The system of American Justice is prejudiced to the rights of life to those who live in areas mostly populated by non whites.
Then when an African American comes to the assistance of others in trouble, there have been incidences where they were shot at or murdered. Murdered because of Ignorance, Prejudice or accident, their murderers (especially if they are white) walked away free.

There are coincidences and over lapping circumstances. There are tragic accidents which do not reflect any homicidal intent.

The problem with the American Justice system is that too many of these cases are exonerated.

Police openly beat Rodney King.

In the future, others will look at the video and admit that they beat on that man with no provocation.

There have been hundreds of incidences were Police have killed unarmed youths, people who had their hands raised or were laying on the ground.

The system wipes its hands on those incidents when they occur to people of color.

If it happens in a white community, it is apologized, memorialized and recognized.

In Black communities it is whitewashed, covered over, argued (never an apology) and never recognized.

In Black communities the priority is to ignore all concerns. To bully and strong arm the residence into accepting the murders as legal.

Tensions were high in Ferguson, Missouri.

Tommy discovered some things which he hadn't known.

In Ferguson, Mo, the police department has fifty three officers, three of which are of African American origin. The town is populated by sixty-seven percent Black residents and twenty nine percent white residents. In Ferguson, similar to the same thing done in New York City, driving/walking while Black is cause for inspection.

In Ferguson, last year, 86% of the stops, 92% of the searches and 93% of the arrests were of Blacks.

The statistics also say that Blacks were less likely to be carrying contraband.

In New York, They found out that over 80% of the stops and frisks were meaningless, they found no reason for the interruption in the lives of the Black citizens.

Black citizens see these unnecessary stops as acts of intimidation and harassment.

White citizens, largely, don't care. They do not feel the pressure and harassment from such unnecessary inspections. Largely, they harbor racist opinions which devalue the opinion and intelligence of African Americans.

Towards the end of the second term for the first African American president, an era marked by the lack of respect from the republican congress (for a Black man as president) and a lack of work accomplished rivaling the worst congressional sessions ever, due to an announced work stoppage by republican leadership.

This was an announcement to the country of racial arrogance.

This is the message they sent out and here it was playing out on the streets.

Ferguson, Mo, is a suburb of St. Louis Missouri.

Gene's uncle lived in East St. Louis.

Tommy had not realized that the city of St. Louis, where the land marked Arch can be found is in Missouri. The city of East St. Louis is across the Mississippi river from St. Louis and it resides in the state of Illinois.

In two days Tommy and Gene would be leaving on their thirteen to fifteen hour trip.

Tommy's focus had started out thinking what he would say to his wife. He needed some definitive decisions to be made. He had worked what he needed to say. He had figured what he wanted to hear. It was all so logical to him but he knew Eloise was going to make the whole thing complicated.

He worked out a plan.

The trip from East St. Louis to California was going to cover more than eighteen hundred and thirty miles.

Straight through driving meant around twenty seven hours.

There were some places which interested Tommy. It is one thing to read about the areas across the country but he was going to have the opportunity to linger a little and experience the sights, sounds, smells and taste.

He was going through Tulsa and Oklahoma City. He would pass through Albuquerque, New Mexico and Flagstaff, Arizona.

There were a couple of national parks and national forests along the way.

Las Vegas was off the beaten path but it could be a pleasant retreat either going to Los Angeles or returning home.

GARRY JOHNSON

The news had Tommy reconsidering his trip alone. He also was leery about his trip to an area going through major social upheaval with a guy who was clearly trouble.

Tommy signaled the bartender.

He had been sitting in a neighborhood bar, a few blocks from his house. He had thought that going out would quiet the voices in his head. The problem was that everything reminded him of his upcoming trip.

The Bartender was a woman named Gail.
Gail was about five feet, two inches of Dark Chocolate. Today she worn a really stylish (Halle' Berry) short haircut.
Her normal hair, which was long (to her back), was tightly packed beneath the very expensive wig.
She experimented with lipstick shades, today it looked peach.

Gail was born and raised in Philadelphia but a few minutes behind the bar and you would swear she was from South Carolina.
Her voice was sugary sweet and she said "Surga" all the time.
"What can I get for you, Surga"?

"Well, said Tommy, I would like to see more of you".
(Tommy looked around the room. It was busy).
"I guess, he continued, that everybody in here would say the same thing". He smiled.
"For now I'll take a double (pointing to his shot glass), another draft (pointing to his empty glass) and bring me some pretzels…please."

Gail seemed to flush as she smiled. She had beautiful large eyes.
She was dressed very stylishly in a red, white and black outfit.
"Anything for you Surga".

Tommy remembers closing a lot of bars. He had his favorite spot close some years ago. He had been in this bar before but was hardly a regular. He heard some of the regulars talking. He missed that.

He was hardly going to enter into any of the conversations, because debating with drunks can get tricky, but he missed those eclectic personalities and obtuse thinkers.

"Here Surga"!

Gail placed Tommy's request before him on the bar. She smiled and winked at him.
Tommy felt warm all over.
He pulled two twenty dollar bills from his pants pocket and placed them on the bar.
Gail reached for one of the bills letting her hand rub against Tommy's hand.
She took one of the bills and looking Tommy right in his eyes said "I'll be back with your change Surga."
She looked Tommy up and down.
"You've been here before, she said. And Surga, if you want to see more of me you're going to have to watch me."

With that being said she rocked backwards and forwards and then she sashayed away.

She was definitely the attraction here.
She worn a short red skirt with black stockings.
On her feet she worn some comfortable looking trail boots.
She walked so elegantly as if in heels.
She had on a white blouse, which was delicately unbuttoned so as to show the glowing skin of her bosom.

Tommy fixated on that sight.
He threw back his head as he emptied his shot glass.
As he took a swallow of his beer, he could hear some of the regulars talking.

There were three men talking.
Two of the men were between 35-40 years old and the third man was a lot older, between 60-75.
There had been a whole lot of discussion and laughter from their area.

One of the younger guys had a head full of hair.

"See man, that's why I carry my shit when I go out. Besides the stupid nigga's, I am not going to let these corporate cops kill me or mine"!!!!!
He patted his leg.

"See Man, replied his cohort, You are the kind of guy who gets stopped."

"We all get stopped, shouted the older man as he slapped the table with his hand."

Gail shouted in her sweet voice, "you guys need me over there."

"You have no idea", said the one with the hair. He was smiling as if he were a Light tower.

"We're okay baby", said the elderly guy.

"Okay, Surga, I'm here for you."
Her voice was so melodic that Tommy focused on it as he took another sip of his beer.

The young guy with the Bald head continued.

"You guys know what I mean. We know that most of the stops and frisks are police profiling. The arrest they make are always categorized as legal or necessary.
He took a gulp of his beer.
They are going to stop you and once they find the gun, they are going to put you in cuffs and charge you with something.
You are probably going to get beat because you are going to tell them how you feel about them and their jobs of intimidation and harassment."

The guy with the hair drank all his beer.
He shouted, "Gail, bring us some more beers"!

He looked at his bald head buddy and senior citizen companions.
"Listen, guys, he spoke, I have to take responsibility for me and mine. I know we have Police and Laws that are supposed to safeguard and protect

my right to life within this country but historically they have failed me and mine.

I am a realist, not an academician, not a politician. I am a citizen who doesn't cheat or kill. They let far too many bad cops/ cops with poor judgments walk free. Them motherfuckers don't care about us."

Gail came over to the table with an ice bucket filled with ice and five cans of beer.

The conversation ended and everyone was focused on Gail.

"Here you go, Surga. I know you men going to take advantage of our special."

"Sure, replied the old timer, while his buddies just sat staring at Gail, Sure, Thanks".

He placed a twenty on the table. "I'll be back with your change, Surga".

As she walked away, the bald headed brother reached into the bucket and pulled out a bottle.
"What is Bohemian ale"?

"Just drink the beer and watch that woman move."

Tommy ordered another round for himself. He was close to his limit. He was lucky to have found this bar on the occasions when Gail was working. He had left the house to break up his pattern.
He had been mildly successful.
He swallowed the shot glass's contents.
He took a big gulp from his bottle of beer.
The bar was busy. Music was playing lightly in the background and there was a huge television which showed Sports News/ Events.
Even the Sports channel mentioned Ferguson, Missouri. Some former and present day players came out in support of the citizens struggle.
The three men at the table continued their conversation. The hairy one said, "As I was saying, I am not given up authority to anyone, especially if they mean me harm.
Shit man, (nodding towards his bald headed friend) not even you.

You give away too much."

Tommy could tell from everything he had heard that the man with the bald head was very analytical and deeply concerned by everything. He took his discussions very seriously.

"I understand where both you young bucks are coming from, said the old man.

I have seen this type thing happen over and over for more years than I want to remember. In fact, I even remember people talking about incidents like these today....... years ago, when I was really young."

"Damn"!!!! replied one of the young bucks

"Yeah, think about that, said the older guy, The real shitty thing about it all is that it still happens today.

Hell, you need to carry a weapon because too many of those white folks are crazy and packing. They would shoot you or I and later say that they were afraid..... we could have no weapons between us and the courts will not punish our murderers as they would us, if the tables were reversed.

Then again if we give into this shit its only going to continue.

It's the logical step in the fight for civil rights.

There is an agenda to relegate Blacks and others of color to the lower rungs of society. Through discriminatory practices they are trying to control those American populations, through economics, unfair housing restrictions, lack of protection from law enforcement and a whole lot of other shit.

(The old guy took a deep breath and big swallow of beer.)

They can't stop us from getting what we want but we have to fight for it.

We shouldn't have to but we do. We can't do it one way. They learned that in the sixties. You have to have legal efforts and community efforts. In the beginning the threats of defense by Malcolm X, The Black Panthers and Stokely Carmichael made dealing with the religious leaders of the south much more desirable. No one philosophy won what came after, they all contributed. And believe me if we don't do what has to be done they will bury us in another facet of slavery.........because believe it or not, most of those white folks are crazy."

The guys laughed and joked. Tommy could hear them clearly.

Suddenly, he heard Gail placing drinks on the counter next to him.

When Tommy focused his real eyes after having enjoyed the room from his mind's eye, he could see Gail smiling brightly and seemingly very excited.

As Tommy turned his head to see who she was beaming at he was suddenly overjoyed.

"Mr. T", said Tommy.

"Can I get you anything else, Surga"?
Gail was twisting from side to side. She unbuttoned another button on her blouse.

"Could you set my friend up again right here, on me."
Terrance spoke in a very mellow tone. Gail seemed to eat every word he spoke.

Tommy and Terrance shook hands.

The two men were good friends.
Terrance had always seen Tommy as the man he wanted to be.
Tommy always saw Terrence as a great example of what other young bucks should be.
The men had enjoyed the luxury and good fortune to have frequented the same community bar which also served as their sanctuary.

Gail was already back refilling Tommy's shot glass. She sat another bottle of beer on the counter next to Tommy's half empty bottle.

"Been awhile", said Tommy.

"Yeah, I have been busy. I have gone back to working on some of my architectural designs and some other art work for the Baxter building downtown. The store is going great......"

"O Wow Surga!!, are you still making those sculptures? I really love your work."
Gail was standing behind the bar looking up starry eyed at Terrence.

GARRY JOHNSON

Both men seemed startled for a moment because neither had actually noticed that Gail was listening to their conversation.

Tommy looked over at Gail's wide eyed attendance and smiled.
He picked up his half empty bottle of beer and drained it.

"Thanks" replied Terrence to Gail.

Another bar patron signaled that he needed Gail's assistance.
She turned her head to acknowledge them and then she turned her head back towards Terrence.
"Surga... if you want anything, just call me."
She winked at Terrence as she walked away.
Drone-like she removed the empty bottle that Tommy had placed back on the bar.

The two men looked at each other and laughed.
"So you still got it Player. Married life has not slowed you down."

"I dated her before, replied Terrence. She was very clingy, as I am sure you can see. We always enjoyed a vigorously playful sex life. We never really ended our relationship.... I just walked away.
    I didn't think that she was here today....... but forget about her. I didn't know that you were here. Whatz up?..... How's Eloise?, what's retirement like? Been anywhere?"

Tommy had so much to say.
It was a relief to actually be able to talk with someone candidly.
There were many subjects that he and Eugene never spoke of.
Terrence was someone he felt more comfortable discussing a variety of subjects and sharing personal revelations.

The friends talked for clearly two more hours.
They laughed and drank. It was obvious that Terrence appreciated Tommy's company as he proceeded plying them both with Alcohol.

It was the first time that Tommy had actually spoken to someone about Eloise and his marriage.

It gave him a sense of where he actually was as he listening to the sound of his voice explain his thoughts.

He had heard everything he said in his head for days. There were times that he thought he was driving himself crazy, rehashing these same thoughts through his mind.

Now as he spoke them he was more confident in them.

He was enjoying life but lonely. He was anxious to travel more and he was open to a new beginning.

Tommy talked about some of the clubs and bars he had been frequenting. There were some juicy stories that he knew Terrence could appreciate.

Terrance listened patiently.

Anyone could tell that he was interested.

He spoke of his concern for Tommy traveling all the way by himself to California.

He knew Eloise had gone to visit their daughter in California but he didn't know that she hadn't returned.

He felt a deep hearted remorse for his brother in spirit.

Tommy had always been an inspiration to him.

Terrence treasured Tommy's opinion because he felt a binding of their souls searching for the same truths.

Terrence had not known many others like Tommy.

In his opinion the world was filled with too many egocentric, unrealistic, uninformed brothers living with their ignorance.

Tommy represented the spirit of hope in the community. He had not gone to college but he was well read. He listened to others, even those who disagreed with him. He formed opinions on credible information and was always offering good advice even to the haters.

Terrence could sense the pain in Tommy's words as he spoke about his marriage.

One thing Terrence knew was that Tommy had a real love for his wife.

There were many occasions when, Terrence, had asked Tommy about marriage. Tommy had been married for ages to the same woman…that was something that Terrence thought impossible, at the time.

There was still something in his voice which spoke of hope.

It reminded Terrence of what he admired the most about Tommy.

Terrence had only been married a couple of years. There were days when he loathed their existence together. He could see that he had been single too long but he wasn't apologizing for it.

The bar was getting crowded, another bartender had come onto duty alongside Gail. It was your basic murmuring crowd but certain loud voices gained attention from time to time.

Terrence looked towards Gail standing at the table where three locals sat.

There was something different about her.

She had changed her clothes.

She now wore Black skin tight leather pants with high heel boots.

Her hair which had been short and auburn when he came in was now long, shiny and Black.

"All this for that jive dude"

Greg was the one talking. He had a head full of hair and he, in Terrence's opinion, was loud, vain and reckless.

"Listen Surga, he's more man than you; and remember nigga' you are married"!!

"So is he"!!!, shouted Greg.

The other guys at the table Jamal, with the bald head and Otis, the elderly one laughed.

"Still better than you, Surga. You're just a hater".!!!

Gail flipped her hair, glanced over at Terrence and walked away from the table.

Greg looked over at Terrence and raised his beer in salute.

Tommy noticed. "What's that"? He asked.

"Just Hens, he said while looking at the three men talk, and Explanations", he said while watching Gail cross the room.

Tommy felt tired. He had been drinking for longer than he had expected. He was hungry. Something was brewing that he didn't need to witness.

Gail walked over and stood right next to Terrence, rubbing his arm.
"Is it true Surga"?
"Yes", replied Terrence

Tommy spoke up quickly, he looked into Terrence's eyes.
"Look good brother, I think I have had it for today. It was really good getting to chat. I am going to turn in and get something to eat before I sleep in front of the television."

Terrence looked at Gail and swiveled his head back to Tommy. She was now holding onto his arm caressing it while she massaged his leg with hers.

"Maybe we can hook up before you go or when you get back, said Terrence. And if you have any problem on the road, call me".

The two men shook hands.

@@@@

THE DAY ARRIVED and the bags were packed.

The evening before they were to leave Gene came over to Tommy's.

Gene was excited and anxious to go. Tommy was prepared for the trip but still working over in his mind what his future beheld.
Gene was happy to have company on the trip.
His uncle was very sick and contemplating death took some steam out of the typical effervescent personality Gene possessed.
Eugene had brought a bottle of Tequila, Vodka and Tennessee whiskey. He stopped by a local sandwich shop and had them make one very large cheese steak, filled with onions, peppers and pickles. The other sandwich he brought was a chicken cheese steak, it was also very large. This sandwich was filled with raw onions, hot and sweet peppers, lettuce and tomatoes.
The sandwiches were each cut into four servings.

Gene is the kind of guy that sometimes even when he agreed with you he could annoy.

Tommy started talking about the Ferguson, Missouri protests. He talked about how the police are too often overzealous when it comes to Blacks.
Tommy thought he could talk some caution and calmness into Gene.

Gene was gobbling down the sandwiches and half of the vodka was gone due to him alone.
Tommy had turned on the radio. WDAS-FM.

Tommy also had prepared a plate of chicken wings, one night, which he reheated and placed on the table with the sandwiches.

He brought four bottled beers and placed them on the table.

First, Eugene started in about them niggers in Ferguson. He intimated that some got what they deserved. Eugene was familiar with many criminal lawyers and listening to their work he formed a sympathetic outlook.

Knowing Eugene well, Tommy just discussed all the discrepancies that are on record and the huge differences of dispensing justice across racial lines. They each had experiences as children and adults.

Next Eugene was berating the police and the criminal justice system. He started raving about the politicians he had met and about how criminal the political process has become.

At this point Tommy thought better of his subject matter.

Eugene was now drunk and upset, because he had vivid memories of things done to friends, family and strangers who were black at the hands of the criminal justice system.

Many of us have these experiences where this country perfectly ruined someone due to the national acceptance of cultural ignorance which cripples racial progress in this country.

The ability to cope with the bullshit of everyday life is one thing but when it is also clouded by lies and malevolent people it can be intense.

Racism has ruined many a good person. It has robbed them of being themselves, it tries to dehumanize and devalue, and when it is done universally, aided by laws and ignorance, it can destroy hope.

Tommy found himself enjoying the food. He knew that many of the things that Eugene was talking about where real to him too.

He wanted him to calm down.

He felt it was better to let him vent.

Tommy walked over to retrieve the television remote.

Suddenly he saw Gene take a disc out of one of the bags he had brought into the house.

"Put this on"!!

Gene raised his arm and presented the disc to Tommy.

It was labeled "Bad Black Ass".

Tommy hesitated a moment. He had never watched a pornographic movie in his house and here he was in the living room.

He thought about what Eloise would say.

She never liked Gene anyhow and presently she was not there.

Even though Tommy had never watched porno at home, he had watched some in various places.

He made sure the blinds were drawn. He then placed some of his favorite music Cd's in rotation.

He knew that the music which was playing was fine.

Gene was not interested in the dialogue of the film.

Tommy brought out some more beers.

The video did take Gene's focus off the corruption in the world.

Basically all he did there after was eat, drink and have several loud vocal outburst's…. like, "Damn!!!! Yea' Go ahead, Go Girl, Did you see that!!!!"

Eventually Tommy fell asleep.

Tommy had wanted to get started in the morning but the hangover kept him asleep until 11:00am.

It wasn't until around 1:30pm that they actually left.

Gene had a morning ritual for days like this.

He pulled out some cocaine.

Tommy was surprised that Gene had not used cocaine last night.

What he found out was that cocaine was a motivator drug. It was a shot of adrenaline to the system.

After breakfast and some snorts of cocaine Tommy was wide awake and ready to roll.

He wondered how much drugs Gene was carrying. He thought about questioning him but reconsidered. Gene knew the dangers and the consequences.

Tommy just had to worry about himself.

Scenery passes by quickly in flashes when you are driving.

You see some things but basically there is only the road and the traffic around you.

Nowadays with GPS navigation you look for landmarks and signs to confirm your directions.

Tommy was sailing along.

Gene had been sampling the stations available through Tommy's satellite radio in the car.

The two men had sang along with the old favorites of R & B.

They vocalized instruments, playing along, with the Jazz greats.

They crooned with the blues. They listened to Underground musical groups and coffee cafe legends. In between the techno dance songs and the hard core & old school rap they covered a lot of ground and saw many sights.

The Pennsylvania turnpike is known as America's first superhighway. In 1884 work was started on a project of tunnels and railway tracks. Troubles plagued the project and in 1935 it was proposed a new concept of a toll road. In 1940 the project was completed. The Turnpike has a length of three hundred sixty miles.

Tommy and Gene traveled three hundred twenty five miles of it before they exited onto the Ohio turnpike.

They had already stopped twice, it was either snacks or restrooms which had halted their journey.

Tommy had decided on laying over in Columbus or Cincinnati for an eight hour rest and a good meal.

He figured Gene would welcome the break.

Already he was planning on checking out the area in St. Louis once we arrived. Gene thought every moment was an opportunity for him to find, woo and bed a woman. He was still nervous about seeing his Uncle Charles.

Tommy thought the diversion of the stop might calm him down and relax his nerves.

Tommy just wanted to rest. He wanted to stop moving on the highway. He wanted to stretch out on a bed and go to sleep.

Gene noticed the look in Tommy's eyes.

"Hey man, let me take the wheel for a little".

At first Tommy didn't acknowledge Gene, he thought he was singing with the music. He was concentrating so hard on the road that he was mesmerized by its traffic flow. The light was turning to dusk and there was still at least a hundred or so miles depending if we were stopping at Columbus or Cincinnati.

"Yo! MAN!!!"

Gene shout echoed in the car.

Tommy straightened up and started talking about his plans to lay over in either Columbus or Cincinnati. He was talking about the differences in distance and the size of the cities when Gene interrupted.

"yeah man, I know have to drive and to get directions from the GPS service. Right now, you better pull your tired behind over into this chair and get some sleep."

Tommy knew that he was right. It was the best thing to do. After all, he would take a short nap and be good on driving what remained.
He pulled the car over and the men exchanged seats.
Gene was all excited. He was grinning broadly.

Tommy snuggled into the seat.
"I am always driving, never sat in this seat."

Gene turned on the Jazz station, within seconds Tommy was on his way to sleep.

Gene took two good snorts of powder into his nose.
"Yeah man, I am used to staying up, (looking at Tommy) you just leave it to me."

5

*T*HERE WAS LIFE *in the film world, all surreal and imaginary.
There was a trip outside of body and mind. It was a time of
serene peace and tranquility. There was no violence, no bad thoughts, only
calm seas.*

*The visions of nature were all around. They whizzed by and came back
again. There was sunlight which was clear yet images that were distorted.*

Soothing sounds carried spirits.

Tommy slowly came to focus. He sat up.

The sign said East St. Louis 45 miles.

They registered at a hotel in St. Louis, Missouri.

In the beginning Tommy thought it would be better than East St. Louis.

*Everything Tommy had read on East St. Louis painted a picture of
impoverishment where he did not want to stay.*

*The area, passing through, East St. Louis was as advertised. There was
a severe level of poverty, with many abandoned buildings.*

*This is the same thing happening to many big cities where blocks of
housing have become abandoned.*

*In this case the landscape of formerly public streets leading into woody
areas where houses and communities had been was vast.*

*The random spotty nature of the existing homes was in some instances
glorious and in another extremely dangerous.*

*Most cities remodel from their interior. The neighborhoods are developed
sporadically. The center cities and downtown areas receive priority.*

The center of St. Louis and East St. Louis were both undergoing some revitalization projects.

In Large cities, realty speculators and financial investors generally swoop up all the properties, in the communities, with massive projects in mind.

There was a smell and look of death here.
Tommy looked out with tearful historical eye.
The lost of industry was all around. It passed as empty blocks where workers had gathered, parked, worked and even dined.
A field which was a parking lot and the abandoned buildings with the faded advertisement barely visible. Overgrown grass, weeds and small trees with areas serving as habitats for wild pets and wilderness vermin.
Trash, abandoned cars. Children playing and exploring the urban jungle. Groups gathered sitting around drinking and smoking, laughing and carrying on. Music pounding, cars gathered, commerce legal and illegal.
Even with the smell and look of degradation there was a joyful peace at its heart.

Tommy still didn't want to be around when things turned bad.

A destitute panhandler came over to the car at a stop light.

Gene was still driving and he waved the man away.
The man backed away. The traffic light had just changed to red. The man was dressed in a disheveled manner.
He worn a coat with many sweaters underneath.
It was a very warm day, his coat was open.
He had a scraggy beard which was peppered black and white.
He looked over the car.
"So you boys from Pennsylvania, uh"?

Tommy reached in his pants pocket and pulled out two one dollar bills.
He reached across to Gene.

Gene saw the money and started complaining.
"Man, don't give these poor ass niggers nothing. Fuck this dude."

The panhandler continued talking, "So you boys is here because of the protest!!! Well I can tell you that we don't need nobody else!
We take our ass whooping and keep on ticking."
He seemed to spit as he talked.

Tommy once again pushed the money over to Gene.

Gene took the money. He looked at the light and then over to the panhandler. He rolled his window down and held up the dollar bills. The light changed to green and Gene slowly took off, raising his third finger.

Gene looked over at Tommy, he knew he had something on his mind and he was going to speak on it but before he did, he said,
"Man, if I had given him this money the cops would be stopping us."

Tommy thought about what Gene had said. He imagined the police coming from out of nowhere and searching them and the car. Tommy tried to quiet his thoughts.
Weather Report was playing on the radio. The song was titled "Bird land".
Maybe Gene was right, he thought.

They were only about fifteen to twenty minutes from the hotel they had picked in St. Louis, Missouri.
Tommy wanted to get out of the car and stretch his muscles.
The inconvenience of being stopped by the police, harassed and searched takes time. Tommy didn't want any delays.
He was still shaking off the remnants of sleep.
He was hungry and needed a change of pace.

The music was fast paced and bouncy.
Gene was echoing the horn parts while Tommy enthusiastically tapped out the drum parts.
Tommy was caught up in the sights of East St. Louis as he drummed. Speechless. Crossing over the Mississippi to Missouri, Tommy continued his wordless activity. The Arch was extremely picturesque.
He had been gradually waking as they made their way to the hotel.

They were almost a day early but the hotel was happy to accommodate. The area had been a center of attraction for all the wrong reasons but it meant visitors and an influx of money to the area.

Gene called his uncle. Tomorrow he would visit which meant tonight they would find some food, get wasted, find some entertainment and explore.

Gene was as ever effervescent to extremes.
He made a few connections and found a couple of spots to visit.
Tommy was impressed.

The navigation system in Tommy's car also gave him suggestions on where to eat.

There were a multitude of Italian restaurants or restaurants offering Italian food.
Tommy settled for a Barbeque restaurant.
They ate prime rib steaks and drank beer to excess.
The decor of the room was rather plain and unmemorable, it was the food that held his attention
Tommy was getting wasted but he tried to remain lucid because now he was driving.
The meat was so tender that they found themselves sucking on the bones, licking their fingers and belching.
Tommy tasted braised rabbit and a wild boar ravioli.
They left this restaurant feeling satisfied but still stopped at a sporting bar and grill.

This was were Gene actually vibrated excitement. The Sporting bar and grill and the last bar they stopped at were lively places.
The music was loud, the patrons were loud.
These were neighborhood bars.

Gene went to the restroom once and returned with two very beautiful women.
The Sporting bar and grill was a vision of an interracial America.
There were people of every hue, laughing, drinking and cavorting.
Football was on most of the screens but one was dedicated to tennis and another to National Hockey preseason.

It was hard to hear the televisions but no one was complaining.

There were nothing but wide eyed and gregarious folks gathered.

The white knuckled, hand wringing gamblers ignored the frivolity occurring around them and sat in silence glued to the images on the screens.

You could tell their moods by the expressions on their faces.

Reading the scrolling text across the bottom of the screens made them react, often increasing their panic.

The last bar they stopped at was really a neighborhood bar.

It was not littered with televisions and it was barely half the size of the Sports Bar and Grill they had left.

The crowd was dressed more casually than the one downtown and even though the room was full of noise, Tommy felt the déjà vu of old familiar haunts in his own neighborhood.

It was late when they left.

Gene had picked up more than women at this stop.

He started snorting and popping pills after his first visit to the men's room.

He was so wasted that the women decided against joining the men at their hotel room.

Tommy was glad. He was also full of inebriates all he wanted to do was go to bed and sleep.

Tommy allowed his navigation system to lead him and Gene back to the hotel.

Once back, he and Gene indulged in a couple of snorts of cocaine before they retired to their separate rooms.

6

*T*OMMY AWOKE IN *a haze.*

This was just what he had expected from Gene.

The night before had produced a cloudy morning, drugging and drinking to the extreme was not something he regularly did or could he maintain.

Gene had already left to visit his uncle and watching television Tommy's day was getting worst.

The morning news on television was really depressing.

The night before, here in Ferguson, a fire was set on the tribute placed in the street to publicize the murder of an unarmed teenager by police.

In Ohio, an innocent teen was purchasing an air gun at a local store. He was not being offensive or a troublemaker. He was not threatening or robbing the store. Police entered the store because they had received a fraudulent complaint. The store camera shows that the teenager did not have the air gun loaded or in his hands when the police shot and killed him. Now this morning Tommy was informed on the news that the local officials failed to indict the officers who murdered the teenager.

There were other published stories of recent police murders of innocent or unarmed black men, women and children.

It was hard to find any legitimate reason for the lack of justice doled out to Black Americans.

It was if the white population wanted to perpetuate the criminal violent behavior against blacks, either forcing them to revolt and be killed or accept the substandard citizenship which they allow.

The reality is that it won't happen.
History shows that Africans were here in America before the colonial forces of the English, French or Spanish.
Blacks have been in this country but never to colonize only as inhabitants and journeyman.
The Europeans came to take over the land and to dispossess all who occupied the it.
The African was and is resilient.
The Europeans, even though they idolized the Indians, were intent on making them their slaves.
The problem was that the Indians fell sick from diseases carried by the European explorers. They could elude the colonialist because they knew the country better and in order to buy time, the Europeans made treaties with certain tribes. This made it hard for Europeans to apprehend those Indians which escaped slavery.
The Indians were used by the English, the French and the Spanish to help each European power gain more land in the America's.
Ultimately the Europeans broke their agreements
The Indian nations and tribes which had numbered thousands, when Europeans landed, became reduced to hundreds.

The import of African Slaves saved the Europeans.
They were ill prepared to undertake the massive job of creating a nation and an economy. The free labor afforded them untold wealth at the expense and lives of the African slaves.
This nation was built on the backs of that free labor and this nation has never apologized or repaid those African slaves.
Reparations are owed.
Descendants of African slaves (American citizens) have been fighting since slavery for fairness and equality of the laws.
White American society has been brutal and vicious in its reply.

Black Americans have endured lynching, political and social disenfranchisement. These actions continue today in one form or another but over the years, African Americans have progressed in ever category possible on the road to acknowledgment and prominence…still there exist and even thrive a hate movement.

It is supported by rich white men who want to control the world.

It is populated by diluted, ignorant and lied to people who will accept any excuse for their failures which doesn't include them.

It doesn't matter though because the world is changing and becoming more intelligent. More people know the real origins of history. Young whites want to distance themselves from the injustices and the stain of racism which runs through their bloodline.

Mixed marriages blur the line.

Injustices keep on occurring and Black America keeps standing for what's right. This will not stop.

What most do not understand is that Black America and the Americans who populate it were born revolutionaries…. not criminals, thieves and liars but revolutionaries. In the true spirit of the constitution pledged by Jefferson, Franklin and Washington, Black Americans stand for all that is good and decent.

This spirit was forged by slaves and will not die.

You subtract the high number of arrest due to profiling and statistics will prove that Black America provides the pluses to our nation not the negatives that the hate groups spread.

Sure there were some negative elements in the black community. Every community has them.

Much of the crime element in the black community was born in reaction to a society where they could not get a job, even when qualified.

Even with this history the black community has not created home grown terrorist or international crime groups like white American has produced and continues to produce.

Tommy's brain was working overtime. Hate has a way of clouding everything else out.

He thought about his relatives and all they had endured so he didn't have to follow in their footsteps. He thought about the injustices he had witnessed on television, in the streets, at work, voting at the polls, shopping and even vacationing.

Tommy walked around his room.

The window from the hotel room overlooked a small sprawl of buildings. Below there were people going about life.

He thought about going out but he was not ready.

Stepping into the shower, the water felt wonderfully refreshing.

The pressures and obstacles in life create an interesting tapestry of colorful and opaque moments and memories.

Tommy wanted to ignore the thoughts and feelings that dealing with racism brought to his life.

It was an extreme blessing that he did not hate all white folks.

He was fortunate to have had a family that had insisted he learn all he could. The historical information in his head concerning race and the pragmatic knowledge gained from living within such a society could ruin a person.

He knew many a person who was bitter and uneasy with the same knowledge. Learning to cope within a racist system is not taught in school and some people are not capable of dealing themselves, so how could they teach.

Tommy grabbed himself.

Maybe, he thought, that he could stimulate himself sexually and forget all about his thoughts on sociology and history.

Memories of the women that he met last night came back to him.

They were enough to bring him to full satisfaction but he preferred real company and not more dreams.

The water continued to pour over him washing away his momentary pleasures. He let the water run down from the top of his head. There was always an achy lifeless feeling he experienced after using drugs. It cleared the cobwebs from his head, initially, but always made his body feel sluggish later.

Still, at this point, he wished he had a little something to clear his head and give him that spark.

He knew that soon he and Gene would part, that would end his access to any drugs. Also he knew that driving alone for the remaining eighteen hundred and forty miles would require his full attention.

It was approaching noontime and Tommy was reconsidering his thoughts of strolling around the city.

He planned to drive to Oklahoma city next and that would take approximately seven and a half hours. He decided to get as much rest as possible and he read the menu for room service.

The menu wasn't as diverse as he might have hoped but he was able to get a salad, a club sandwich, some chicken wings and beer.

He also knew that he and Gene would probably go exploring again tonight before they left going their separate ways tomorrow.

He needed to put some food into his system.

Tommy was a thinker. He was a television watcher of various types of programming.

He had never attended college because he had to work but he was always pushing the envelope trying to find information to educate his mind.

At home he had the ability to peruse a multitude of channels.

In this hotel room there were not as many options.

News programming, Talk shows, DIY programming and movies or television shows which he had already seen filled the airways.

It was close to three in the afternoon when Gene came knocking on the door.

"Damn Man, you in here watching football highlights. I know they have a skin channel with more action, I watched it last night."

Tommy smiled. He had been watching football highlights but they were also talking about spousal abuse and the leagues new policies.

The world was changing and athletes and their off field behavior was being scrutinized much more than ever before. It was a good thing but it bothered Tommy that people asked more of their hometown athletes then they did of their elected officials.

It appeared that so many of the elected officials were selling out their constituencies for corporate dollars. The average elected representatives campaign one way and occupy their office completely opposite. It was maddening.

In Tommy's mind, Gene offered some relief from such heavy thoughts.

Gene reached into his jacket pocket and produced two marijuana cigarettes and a small bag of cocaine.

He motioned at one of the unopened beers on the table.

Tommy nodded approvingly.

Gene sat down at one of the chairs for the table.

He sighed and appeared heavy in a unique mood. He was Quiet.

Gene picked up the joint and lit it. He took a long drawl of the weed and passed the joint to Tommy.

Without speaking, holding in the smoke, he opened the cold can of beer. He paused and blew out a big cloud. Then without speaking he gulped down the beer.

Tommy was also quiet.

He knew that Gene's uncle was family and brought memories of the past. A past which placed Gene in a melancholy.

He had been uncomfortable coming to East St. Louis alone.

Tommy had felt an obligation as a friend to come along.

He had his own mission but he felt in his heart that doing Gene this favor was part of the buddy oath.

Yesterday when Gene called his uncle and realized that he would be going to meet his uncle alone, it shook him. His uncle insisted that he come to the nursing facility alone, that there were some important papers and information he wanted to talk about.

It was the reason Gene got so wasted the night before.

Had Gene not been dreading to see his uncle he undoubtedly would have brought the women back from the bar.

He was not himself then and he was quiet now.

Tommy could only imagine that Gene's visit was traumatic.

Tommy took another pull on the joint and handed back to Gene.

Without looking, Gene reached over took the joint and silently took another drawl.

He coughed a little. A big smile came over his face.

"Man, you will not believe this shit. This was one crazy, motherfucking day."!!!!!!

It was an hour and a half straight without pause and very little interruption, that it took for Gene to tell his story.

He started quietly with a lot of description and ended loudly with incredulous laughter.

The visit to his uncle had been a pleasant experience, at least, in the beginning.

The facility was in Illinois outside of the city of East St. Louis.

It was, as described by Gene, on a sprawling green complex.

They had a spacious high rise apartment facility, an adjoining entertainment facility with three movie theaters with screens large enough to play major movies.

They even had a large banquet room where they held group meetings, food banquets and Dances.

There was a stage where they could have live plays performed or which served as the bandstand for musical groups.

He said that they had a park behind the High rise which offered a real picturesque view for the apartments above.

There was a walking and jogging path surrounding a wooded area with nature trails.

There was a tennis court area and even an area for Basketball and Volleyball.

The facility was either recently built or just very well maintained.

Gene had been thoroughly impressed by the nursing home, the amenities and knowing that his uncle was so fortunate.

Gene had expected to find his uncle bedridden but he was seated in the lobby area on the floor where his apartment was. He had been waiting for the housekeeping crew to finish in his quarters.

Uncle Charles was dressed like he had been playing golf.

There was a Golf course bordering the nursing complex but Uncle Charles was not physical capable of indulging.

Uncle Charles used a cane and he showed Gene around his apartment. Gene was again impressed because he said his uncle had a large suite.

There was a huge bedroom with a spectacular view of the landscape. The furniture was classic and very well made.

Gene could see that the bedroom was equipped with outlets and levers where oxygen or whatever gases are needed can be supplied.

The bathroom was large enough to allow maneuvering of three wheelchairs doing synchronized dance moves.

All of the rooms had high ceilings but none higher than the living room area.

There were two different reclining chairs in the room, "both were extremely comfortable" Gene added. There was a long sectional sofa. All of the chairs were covered in very soft leather.

Uncle Charles reminisced about the past. He talked to Gene about his sister, Gene's mom. He talked about his feelings when Charles died. Uncle Charles had some snapshots of those days and he shared them with Gene during the visit.

Gene seemed to tear up a little discussing his uncle's memories but with a momentary pause, a hardy snort of powder / a good puff and he continued unfazed.

There were personal effects that he wanted to give Gene now.

He was arranging for Gene to get the proceeds from the sale of his house, there was mint condition 1977 mustang convertible and a couple of boxes of memorabilia which he would have shipped to Gene.

Uncle Charles explained to Gene that he had suffered from some horrible injuries working in the prisons and that he had other ailments (such as diabetes, high blood pressure, gout, prostrate cancer and lung cancer) which affected his eyes, his daily stamina and mobility, his hearing and his equilibrium.

Uncle Charles sadly told Gene that he had been diagnosed to die within a year.

The medication that his uncle was taking could have been responsible for the long conversation which followed, at least that's what Gene said.

Uncle Charles said that he had become friends with some super ultra-military men who also worked at the prison.

He talked about how that association was responsible for him being housed in such a luxurious nursing/living facility.

"You know, said Gene, I never even noticed."

Uncle Charles told him to look around, there were ten to twelve Black people living in this facility. The facility housed close to three thousand occupants.

He said he knew some very high level players and how things in the future would change. Uncle Charles explained how there were/are quasi-military forces which are mobilizing, gaining assets, stockpiling weapons and gaining influence across the country and even the world.

This was where Gene laughed a lot and insinuated that his uncle was out of his mind.

Uncle Charles talked about local and national elections. He said that he was a member of a group which had candidates running for various offices, in various states. He predicted a new world order, here in the United States, run by coalitions determined to reconstruct the government, federal guidelines and even State borderlines.

Gene was laughing too hard to fully describe the new financial standard which his Uncle's conservative buddies were going to establish. He considered the whole thing a pipe dream for old world beaters.

Uncle Charles wanted Gene to know what was going on because he wanted Gene to benefit from the relationship, after all, they were family.

Tommy felt that Uncle Charles must have exerted some extraordinary influence on Gene because he never told his Uncle what he really thought. He was expressing his thoughts now.

"Can you imagine, Gene said, Me and a room full of right wing conservative assholes?!!?
They would pull out their guns and shoot me on the spot.
Those old Motherfuckers been too deep into their medication.

My Uncle wants me to come back in a month and meet some people......
Tommy do you hear this shit".!!!!!

Gene took another snort.

Uncle Charles explained to Gene that the group he was in wanted new blood and they were hoping to incorporate more people of color.
Uncle Charles thought that Gene's legal background and Banking contacts would be a perfect fit.
This group of conservative members wanted Gene and other professionals like him to spread their doctrines around the country getting other Blacks to support their agendas.

The main premise of their philosophy was that Life and Freedom are commodities. Uncle Charles mentioned Democratic Republic but it basically sounded like an Oligarchy where a few people (who believe they are special, Royal or wealthy) claim some divine right to decide realty for everyone else.

Gene said that they had lunch delivered to the room.

Uncle Charles talked randomly, said Gene.
He spoke out against President Obama and what he saw as the abysmal way he ran the country.
Gene laughed as he talked about it all.

Uncle Charles gave him the information where to pick up the car.

Gene took a taxi to the location and collected the vehicle.

He was ecstatic about the car. It had a shimmering blue paint job and drove like a dream.
Gene said he couldn't wait to test it on the highway home.

"But the Big Thing that really blew my mind, continued Gene, was that when I looked in the trunk there was a huge case."

"And what was in the case"? asked Tommy, happy to have a voice.

"Well, said Gene, it contained two semi-automatic rifles and three handguns"...(there was a quiet moment)

Then Gene shouted...... "Can you believe this Shit"!!!!!!!!!!!

7

*T*HIS HAD BEEN *a day full of heavy thoughts and revelations.*

Gene's experience with his uncle merely placed the water way above the rim.

Tommy accompanied Gene to the sparkling blue mustang.
He inspected the trunk and found exactly what Gene had confessed with the addition of two magnificent Bowie knives and one dangerous looking machete.
After persuading Gene to leave the car safely parked in the hotel lot, the two men decided to enjoy a night of divine frivolity.

There are times when bad news, rotten weather or a series of mishaps foretell worst things to come. It was obvious that the there had been and continues to be great injustices occurring to African American citizens. As Black men Gene and Tommy have had to find ways to cope. The problem is that issues of race are prevalent in the United States. Therefore, Black people have an extra burden and that is dealing with life in general (were you meet all kinds of people) and dealing with those who are produced, affected or perpetuating racism.
Coping with life is difficult for most people of any racial background. The extra burden that Black Americans face in America is produced and assisted with a blind eye by our government.

This night was something to wash the troubles away. It started after Gene finished explaining his trip to see Uncle Charles.

He made some calls from his room.

Tommy decided to stretch his legs and walked to a near by liquor store.

There he picked up some more beer and two bottles, one was vodka and the other was tequila.

The liquor store was close enough to walk to and far enough away to give him time to think.

The fresh air felt rejuvenating. For a moment Tommy was allowed to let his mind travel away from his thoughts. He walked wide eyed and alert to the sounds, smells and people around him.

There was a couple arguing in a car. It paused for a moment in the street. Other cars went around them. The couple each got out a verbal assault and then a woman stepped out of the car.

She slammed the door, walked cautiously to the curb and entered a convenience store on the corner.

She walked with a degree of composure and purpose. She was mad and it showed.

The driver, a man, was still talking and smacking his steering wheel, then he decided to park.

Tommy was walking slowly and he took notice of their argument.

He thought of how fragile and full of passion relationships become. Was he headed towards that type of reunion with Eloise?

He had spoken to his daughter and Eloise a week ago. He had not mentioned driving out there, he was going to mention that in a day or so. He thought he would do that when he was in New Mexico or Arizona.

He had been so undecided concerning the trip. He felt he knew her response but he needed her reaction, face to face. He needed to get on with his life.

Tommy walked on to his destination.

He bought the Liquor and beer.

On the return trip back to the hotel, Tommy passed by the driver, who was caught up in the argument, standing outside his car.

He was patting his foot and mumbling to himself.

A glance and the men acknowledged each other.

"Damn Women!!! Frustrating a Brother, always making shit difficult", said the driver.

"I know the feeling, replied Tommy, I know the feeling."

Gene was back in his room. He said he wanted to take a shower and make a couple of telephone calls.

The hotel was busy with visitors. It was 6:30pm.

Tommy went back to his room to drop off a couple of beers.
He wondered what Gene's mood would be after discussing his uncle.
He wondered what he would say about the issue himself.
How much of what Uncle Charles said could be dismissed?
Tommy read a collection of magazines each month and what he was talking about wasn't too far fetched, now if he was a part of something or if it was all in his mind, that was another matter.

Gene's room was opposite Tommy's. He stepped out through his door took two footsteps across the hallway and tapped on Gene's door.

Gene poked his head out.
Tommy took a step forward but Gene was slow to move.
"Hey Man… just checking" he said.

Now someone was moving behind Gene coming for the door.

Gene stood back and Tommy saw a very shapely woman with long black hair that fell between her shoulders in a "V" shape. Her eyes sparkled and so did her fingernails.
She wore a tight lime green blouse that showed off all her goodies. She wore daisy duke shorts, which accentuated her big legs and she wore no shoes.
"Hey.. I'll check with you later", she said.

She gave Tommy at glance as she left.

She pranced down the hallway on her toes and disappeared around a corner.

"Close your mouth" said Gene and he motioned for Tommy to step in.

Tommy placed the booze and beer on the table careful not to interfere with the area Gene had already set up as a work space for rolling joints and snorting cocaine.

Gene returned with two glasses from the counter in the bathroom.

He placed ice in the glasses from a full ice bucket on the stand next to his bed. He was pouring himself some vodka when Tommy said, "Okay man, where did she come from? Damn how the hell did you do that? I wasn't gone that long."

Gene laughed. "You know, when you're hot, you're hot. I went to the ice machine and I met her. We came back here".

Gene finished pouring the vodka and started to drink. He pointed to a rolled joint on the table. Tommy picked it up and lit it.

Gene continued talking.

"You know she's coming back. She is here with her girlfriend who stayed here while passing through town. Her name is Judy and she lives here in St Louis."

Tommy couldn't believe how effortless Gene made single life look.

Sure he had bad days but his good days were spectacular.

Tommy was so cautious and it showed. Women were unsure about him because he exerted his caution loudly.

Gene was open and loud. He was attracted to all women as a conquest and he made the women feel good being played.

He was full of compliments. He worked hard making women interested in him.

This was what Tommy was going to have to develop if he wanted to swing in his old age. Tommy had too much respect for everyone. He felt an obligation to be truthful and sincere. At times it could be said that he was too serious.

Tommy knew these things about himself but they were difficult for him to change.

Gene had little respect for anyone and he had never pledged to be honest, truthful, serious or sincere. He would lie in a moment of casual conversation as easily as he would lie if ever interrogated.

Whenever women were involved Gene would do or say anything for a new sexual hook up. He never worried about the woman's feelings or age. Every women was fair game if she was in the game with him.

Gene was a man of many vices. Women and Drugs were at the top.

In his mind the world was a giant battlefield and you were either a soldier or a citizen of an occupied city.

He saw Tommy as a reluctant soldier. In his mind, Tommy was a behind the lines support person instead of an out front fighter. They had been bound together by the spirit of his dead brother. Over the years their own friendship had grown but it was one of support and entertainment.

They were different as night in day about so many things but that never stopped them from enjoying themselves together.

Tommy was more a drinker than a druggie but together they indulged as kindred spirits.

The experience they had in Atlantic City had shown them both how they fed off of each other.

Gene was drawn to Tommy's wisdom. Even if he thought many of the things he said were hokey, he came to realize that he was extremely knowledgeable. He found a strength of conviction and satisfaction / calmness in Tommy's demeanor.

The knowledge that Gene had of the world actually frightened him. He found that soldiering up, going pre-emptive suited him.

In his mind it was better to hurt than be hurt. He knew people responded to pain but he was less aware that they responded to reason.

In Tommy's presence, Gene felt empowered.

Tommy had a calm way of talking and presenting arguments or his opinion. He used silence to his advantage. He could diffuse tense
Situations through knowledge.

Gene was a loud out front, cursing and swearing person who used intimidation and abrasiveness to establish his desires. Most people who came in contact with him either ignored him, fought him or found his crudeness endearing.

This was the dynamic of these two man's friendship.

They talked, laughed and imbibed on all levels.

Tommy was soaking in the nuance of his freedom.

He was prepared to being open to new ways to live, new people and circumstances outside of his routine. He was blasted. He knew this was one of those times when he was living outside of his routine. If he was lucky he would have fun, meet people and get away without making any bad decisions. If he was unlucky he would wind up in serious trouble.

Tommy lived on pleasant thoughts. He knew bad things happened and he felt prepared to handle most. He lived on an optimistic plain where rarely would he consider violence, be it, pre-emptive assaults, defensible physical / mental attacks or retaliation for attacks suffered or feared.

He had always tried to maintain that demeanor and as he had gotten older the percentage of positive results increased.

If he had been a more aggressive thinker he would have realized that Gene was an anomaly. He would have realized that once he added Gene to the equation he would have to re-do the problem and receive a new answer.

There are times when you know trouble is around the corner.

Gene had made telephone calls to one of his contacts.

He had several associates from South Philadelphia with whom he had made a life long connection.

Prostitution, drugs or gambling were their specialties. He had established a contact to get some more drugs for the night.

Women were not going to be a problem and if they were he still had options.

True to form and befitting Eugene's luck with woman, Judy returned with a much taller and statuesque beauty named Denise.

The drugs were delivered within an hour when Tommy and Gene and the ladies were preparing to head out through the city.

This delayed the journey for another hour.

It was such a synchronous occasion. Everything seemed to perfect for words.

The women, Judy and Denise, were gorgeous. The cocaine Gene received was more potent than the product he had before and the women produced some marijuana which also surpassed the product Tommy had tasted earlier.

The coalescence of such signs would sometimes herald caution.

There was no caution in Gene's game and Tommy might have known better had he not wanted such a distraction.

Judy had a car. She knew the city, she insisted on showing the men around town.

Bells were ringing but Tommy could not hear.

8

*I*T WOULD BE *difficult for Tommy to recall everything he saw that night or where he went.*

He would beat himself up later because he was too open, carefree and forgiven taken into account he was in uncharted waters.

Then again he would acknowledge his faith in God as his shield.

The areas of the city and the surrounding suburbs whizzed pass his vision. Tommy sat in the rear of the Black Mercedes sedan with Denise.

Both women seemed adapt at describing and calling out landmarks but little stuck in Tommy's brain. If it had he would have recalled that St. Louis Missouri was mentioned as one of the five most dangerous cities in the country. He would have also remembered to stay away from Washington Park and that Police harassment, intimidation and murder were legendary in the area.

If Tommy had been lucid he would have been suffering from the deja' vu recalling a youth dealing with the racist Philadelphia police department and the corrupt criminal justice system they supported.

Gene was loud and commanded much of the conversation with everyone in the car, especially Judy. It appeared that he was well on his way to bedding another fair maiden. It was a game where neither one was innocent.

Tommy and Denise spoke little to each other but all the communication was pleasant. It appeared to Tommy that she was also trying to have a good time by pushing more troubling thoughts away. He could understand.

They passed drugs back and forth and as the night progressed it included touching and sitting closer together.

How many bars did they visit? Tommy remembers two houses, one of which was a bar.

He later recalled the conversation of some of the people he met that night.

There were moments and memories which stood out but they were cloudy. There was also the notion that even if St Louis was west of Philadelphia that Tommy was around southerners. The language and viewpoints must have traveled up the Mississippi. Tommy could recall the southern drawls.

He met a guy named Messy. Messy was a someone the women knew. He joined them at a rickety table in one of the bars. He laughed and joked with everyone, swapping tall tales with Gene.

What Tommy remembered best was when Messy talked about going to a funeral for some relatives in Alabama. He talked about how it was always difficult and strange returning home.

Messy's uncle Jess was a family enigma. He was basically a poor vagabond traveling throughout the state. He always seemed to come back home, to a town called Demopolis, where most of his family resided in Alabama.

Uncle Jess was a man of many different personalities. He claimed to have followers and a group of disciples everywhere.

He claimed to have walked the whole length and width of the state numerous times in an effort to heal the land.

Well, one day in a tent he lived in near the Black warrior river, he was found dead.

The family was going to have him cremated because money was tight but word of mouth brought in some donations and one white man from Selma donated twenty five thousand dollars so more of Jess's followers and family could attend his funeral.

Uncle Jess's funeral was attended by thousands of people from every walk of life.

It was apparent that Uncle Jess knew a lot of people and that many people knew him or of him.

The ceremonies were held outside at a site nearby to where he died.

Messy described how his Uncle was dressed in a suit with a tie and shoes. Many of his family had never seen him dressed so formally alive. Everyone remarked how good he looked for a dead man.

It was a very hot Alabama day and Messy said that they wanted to bury Uncle Jess quickly because due to his wishes he was not treated by a licensed undertaker.

Jess said that the family was joking that they had to bury him before the smell of him buried them.

Well before they closed the casket after the last viewing, many of Uncle Jess's friends gathered around the casket and sprinkled and placed all types of wildflowers, weeds and foliage in the casket covering Uncle Jess.

Messy stopped and drank down a full mug of beer before continuing. Gene was getting antsy and if Messy didn't end his story soon Gene would have.

"Well, Messy continued, in his Saint Louis drawl, After two minutes of the sermon, the casket shook violently and suddenly up popped the lid of the casket and there Uncle Jess sat smiling and chewing on some of the plants covering him.

The family and other members of the funeral jumped up screaming and running for the hills. I was busy helping one of my female cousins who fainted on the spot.

Several of Uncle Jess's followers helped him out of the casket and within minutes they were gone."

It was uncomfortably quiet for a few seconds and then everyone erupted in disbelief.

"Get the Fuck out of here"!!!!! was the general consensus.
Messy objected vehemently.

"I saw him rise", he shouted. My aunt, his sister, nearly had a heart attack and she is plagued by nightmares of her brother visiting her. She loved her brother but it was unnatural and she's afraid that the spirit that took him will come and take us all."

Tommy remembers trying to be logical.
"Why is she afraid that it is something evil"?

"Its Bullshit"!!! shouted Gene.

GARRY JOHNSON

The ladies were laughing and kept requesting Messy to "shut up and go get sober"!

It was a crowded little drinking spot and the commotion made the drinking crowd turn to see what the trouble was.
In some cities, the ruff riders tough guy mentalities still exist.
The St. Louis area is known to have gangs and gang affiliations.
Tommy remembers the faces glaring at his entourage.
Gene had told Messy to "get the fuck out of here" and it seemed that some of the locals took offense at their hometown boy being dissed.

A very short man came over to the table. He appeared to be somewhere in his thirties. Tommy was bad with guessing and in his present state he was even more unsure, but he ventured that the guy was younger than he or Gene.

"Hey Pops!!!, where you from"?

Gene looked at him and laughed, "We're from Philadelphia, Mr. Baggins".

"My name ain't Baggins, old head.!! We don't preciate you fucking with our boy Messy. I knew you was from so other place or you would have known that."!!

Gene looked down on the man and looked around the room, checking eyes and movements.
"Listen Howard the Duck, if I need your help, advice or 'small talk', I will call."
Judy and Denise jumped up and suggested they leave.
Gene wanted to play a hard sell but once Judy placed her hand on his crotch he was putty in her hands.

On the way out the short thug spoke, "Yeah that's right and remember I can always come to Philly to whip your ass."

"I think there's a city ordinance against midgets", replied Gene while in tow of Judy.

There was some discussion in the car. The women were hungry and drunk. Denise reminded Judy that she had to travel to Oklahoma city and how she still had to make those arrangements.

That was when Gene interrupted and said "Tommy is driving there tomorrow, he can take you."

After that announcement and a nod of commitment from Tommy the group started to laugh again and proceeded off to get some food.

The weather had been cloudy and windy. There was talk of storms and heavy rain. Tornado alerts were a constant fixture, either running across the bottom of the television screen or breaking into radio and television programming.

Somehow the group settled in at a restaurant which specialized in barbequed foods.

This was when Tommy remembers things becoming clearer.

He had agreed to take Denise to Oklahoma city and now she was telling him her story.

She had been born in Charlotte, North Carolina but her family moved to the St. Louis area when she was young.

Her parents died in a gas leak explosion at their home. That was when she started living with her childhood friend Judy.

Three years ago she left St. Louis to explore her birthplace of Charlotte and she stayed there.

She said that she had discovered family still living in the area. There in Charlotte she escaped the lunacy of the conditions present in St. Louis.

She had come back to St. Louis because of some personal loose ends and after she completed her business in Oklahoma city she was heading back to what she called the sanctity of her small southern home.

The restaurant was not a black establishment and it was in a more diverse community. The patrons in the restaurant were basically white but other customers of color sprinkled the basic Caucasian diners.

There were televisions on opposite walls offering entertainment, news and sports to the dining room areas.

GARRY JOHNSON

Gene was still romancing Judy. He whispered sweet phrases in her ear and smothered her constantly with compliments.

Tommy had felt the need to reduce his alcoholic intake but Gene and Judy continued consuming without pause.

The food at the table was phenomenal. There were slabs of ribs and a whole barbequed chicken. There were several ears of corn on the cob in melted butter, baked potatoes, spinach cooked in butter and garlic. Fantastic dinner rolls. There was a large pitcher of imported beer and the waitress continually removed empty glasses of liquor.

The food was delicious.

Tommy felt as he had not eaten for days

There was a bar area in the restaurant where people gathered and watched the sports highlights.

Weather alerts and news alerts concerning the ongoing protests flashed across the screen constantly.

A booming voice echoed throughout the restaurant from the bar.

"Burn the Flag!!!! send those monkeys back to Africa. They don't like it here, they can leave. I'm tired of these bastards always asking us to give them something. Get a job Dumb Niggers!!"

Gene jumped up.

"If their Government does not serve them, they have a right to protest, burn the flag or shit on the Police departments steps. Those dumb bastards would work if you fucking bigots didn't discriminate. At least they are not shooting unarmed children and trying to cover it up"!!!

There was already some effort at the bar to silence the congregation of unruly white drinkers from where the initial complaint came.

After Gene's little speech there was a rustling of chairs.

The bar crowd acted as if they were going to advance.

That was when Tommy stood up.

"If you think those people out there are being treated fairly with respect and justice then you are blind and ignorant."!!

Now the wait staff and management was coming into the aisles trying to comfort and restrict both sides from advancing.

One waiter approached Gene,
"listen, said Gene, I came in here to eat. I am spending my money not his and I don't want to hear Willie Lynch."

"I'm sorry sir, I'm sorry" was all the waiter could say.

"Listen old timer, I'll whup your monkey ass"!!

"I've heard that before, replied Gene, but here I stand telling your dumb cracker ass..... FUCK YOU!!!!!!"

The patrons in the restaurant were silent but many looked like they were prepared to hit the floor to escape any bullets which could start flying.

Management was trying to disperse the bar crowd. They tried to get everyone standing seated and to stop the flow of words across the facility.
Meanwhile, the waiters were trying to do the same at the table where Gene and Tommy were standing.

Once again Judy insisted that they leave. Once again Gene protested until Judy placed her hand on his thigh.

Management apologized for the trouble and packed the remainder of the meal on the table into Styrofoam containers. All gratis.
They even included a six pack of beer and accompanied us to our car. They did not want any commotion on their property.

Adrenaline was flowing in the car.
The conditions in the area provided a low warm front with cloudy skies and an occasional cool wind.
The car windows started fogging.

Gene was still spouting about 'white folks' and Tommy was still excited / stimulated about the fight they almost had and the shouting match they just participated in.

Judy gave Gene a big kiss to shut his mouth and Denise wrapped her arms and body around Tommy.

It was impossible to see through any of the car windows and they all laughed.

They drove cautiously to the hotel. They all realized that they might be confronted by the bigots from the bar or that Police answering a call about the incident in the restaurant might come and harass them. It was a giddy kind of quiet which traveled with them.

They could barely wait until they were in the hotel and able to continue their party.

9

*I*T RAINED ALL night. The wind was howling outside of the hotel windows while the rain beat against the glass.

Tommy lay in the bed wrapped by the covers and covered by warm, soft flesh.

He and Denise had spent the night consummating their liaison.

They had started out in Gene's room drinking, drugging and reliving their night together.

It became blatantly obvious when Gene and Judy stripped off all their clothes and jumped into bed that it was time for Tommy and Denise to leave.

One thing in common about Tommy and Gene was that even if they were seniors they never acted like it.

The mental reality that they were both over fifty years old remained in their heads.

Tommy was poor at predicting age.

He figured that Denise was over forty. There were wrinkles which he could have misdiagnosed but he thought he might be on the right track. She had a basically firm body even though there was bouncing flesh on her bones. She excited him.

Many aspects of life have been bastardized in modern society.

There is fear that eating out places the consumer in danger of consuming inferior meat and produce products doctored up to look, smell and taste good.

There is danger that a trip to the local movie theater, or an outdoor musical or sporting event could end with the audience dodging bullets.

The beauty of the human form that has been so well documented in Art has been surpassed by the numerous illicit pornographic images displayed in any media form you pick.

There are those who have lost their will and minds by becoming so saturated by the pornographic images that they have destroyed the pure joy, satisfaction and exhilaration which honest sexual contact bring.

Many people have lost that frame of mind where sexual contact is beautiful because they are filled with the indecent violent brutal one sided search for gratification at any cost.

Tommy was extremely stimulated by the hours of love making that he and Denise had engaged in before falling fast asleep. In the wee hours of the morning they both participated in mutually satisfactory sexual stimulation and gratification which left them exhausted and very happy.

It was possible that they both were relieving tension and emotions which had been pent up for some time.

Regardless, Tommy felt extremely comfortable pressing his naked flesh against hers and her responses lead him to believe that his efforts were welcome.

It was 10:45am. It was raining heavily outside. The beads of water ran down the windowpane distorting the view of the outside.

Tommy squeezed Denise's body once more, rubbing her lusciously firm legs with his leg.

He softly separated himself from her. She made a soft cooing sound as he moved away.

He looked at her body as he placed the cover over her before he moved to the bathroom.

This was one of those times when he definitely felt his age.

This was not his normal pattern and he had not been taking his regular medication, minerals and vitamins.

The cocaine severely interacted negatively with his body as it lost its anesthetic properties. Luckily he had eaten or his condition would have been worst and that would have affected his sexual performance. As it was he gamely walked into the bathroom to relieve himself.

Looking at himself in the mirror he smiled.

He and his wife, Eloise, had not had sex for over half of their married life. The last time was well over fifteen years ago.

Thinking of the beautiful body in the bed his manhood jumped with excitement. He had never lost his feelings for Eloise but she had denied his advances on ever occasion and he had come to accept that their sexual life was over. He missed that feeling.

He was not sure why he and his wife had ended their sexual life, he surely had not said or implied that he didn't want it. She had made the decision without his input and that was something he hated. Had he done anything so personal or intimate to her, she would have screamed foul. His complaints, meanwhile, were not even acknowledged.

She wanted to hold him to a marriage she had abandoned.

This was why he was making this trip.

Tommy opened his pill bottles and proceeded to swallow them with a cup of water. His body was tired.

He decided to step into the shower.

The warm water once again invigorated his body.

He started to consider if the weather was too intense to travel through. He was well aware that he was going to be traveling through tornado country.

He needed to decide because within an hour or so he would be obligated either to extend his room reservation or find somewhere else to wait out the heavy rains.

The door to the bathroom opened.

"Hi Baby". Denise's voice was a little gravely sounding.

She pulled back the heavy shower curtain and stepped in.

The area was large enough for four people.

Denise took the soap out of the dish and started to lather up.

Tommy could not help containing his excitement and she noticed.

GARRY JOHNSON

She started to rub him over with a soapy facecloth. It felt good and only increased his excitement and by the look in her eyes it excited her too.

"I was thinking of extending my check out time because of the heavy rain. I don't know if you have any specific time that you have to be in Oklahoma city…but.. I'm just trying to be safe."

Its was hard for Tommy to concentrate as Denise make a thick lather of suds which she spread from her body to his by rubbing bodies.

"That's not a bad idea", she said,(as she bent over forward using the cloth to wash between his legs), "I will have to check out of the room I rented", she continued.

All Tommy could see was the contour of her back and two cheeks which he wanted to grab.
At this point his manhood sprung to attention.
She caught it in her soapy hand and stroked it.

Tommy closed his eyes and drifted into a blissful ecstasy.

"When I get back, we're going to remedy this", she said with a bouncing movement. She placed her finger in her mouth.
She rinsed off and stepped outside the shower.

Tommy stayed in the running water. He was spent physically and felt the need to wash all over again.
Denise dressed and left to retrieve her belongings. She blew Tommy a kiss, winked her eye and patted her hip as she left the room.

Tommy called down to the front desk to see what arrangements he could make. It was cheaper to just register the room for another day than to extend arrangement for a few more hours.
The front desk said that their reports were that the weather would clear around three or four in the afternoon.

Tommy then called Gene's room.

"Yeah.. Yeah…!!! Who is it"!! shouted Gene.

"Its me Man"

"Everything alright Man"

"Sure, I just extended my room for another day. I think its raining too hard to travel right now."

"Uh huh, replied Gene, You still taking Denise with you"?

"Yeah, replied Tommy, she has gone to check out of her room now but we will be leaving later. I will either leave later today or tomorrow morning."

Tommy could tell that Gene was distracted.
He could also tell that Judy was still there because Gene said something to her while Tommy was speaking to Gene.
Gene started laughing and then he continued,
"That's good man, look I'm just hanging out here with Judy. We are going to hit the streets soon. You guys can come, but if you've got other plans go ahead. If we miss you guys leaving just remember to be careful. Hell Brother, we had a hellava time here."

"You remember to be careful, responded Tommy. Be careful in that car and remember what you've got in the back."

"No sweat, replied Gene, got it handled. And pound that….. (there was the sound of a slap) What's wrong with you girl?!?...... O' Yeah, Tommy I gotta go. See you back in Philly."

Tommy signed off. It was obvious Gene and Judy were being very playful and probably sky high.

Tommy checked the supply of goodies they had on the table in the room. There was a half of a chicken and several rolls. There were about three bottles of beer and three rolled marijuana cigarettes.

Tommy was walking around in the buff but he decided to put on a light pair of sweatpants and a shirt.

He turned on the television but didn't see anything he wanted to be involved with.

He switched on the radio in hopes of finding some good music to groove on until Denise returned.

He was still excited by her last touch and he was like an addict.... he wanted more.

Going up and down the radio frequencies Tommy couldn't find what he was looking for but he settled on a talk station when he heard a familiar sounding voice.

Whoever the caller was he was soliciting for reason and uniformity.

He said that he was disgusted by all the talk. Apparently callers were giving all manners of details of the recent shooting that were not verified or substantiated. He felt that possibly everyone had been jumping to judgment. It was obvious to him that many of the white citizens were blindly on the Police Officers side.

He tried to explain that he was trying to remain open to the truth but that this would not be the first Police Officer who lied to protect his job.

He felt that the crucial element was that once the teenager was leaving the scene that the officer acted inappropriately.

There was a lot of squawking which followed. There were some inappropriate name calling and questioning of one another's sanity. In essence many of the white locals called the teenager a thug and confessed that he got what he deserved.

Even the radio commentator sounded bias but he allowed the first speaker to continue.

This speaker, who Tommy believed was black, continued by saying that regardless of any of the extraneous comments were he felt were unfounded that the basic issue was the officers conduct.

He started by trying to sympathize with the hard and dangerous job which is police work. He said that Police are trained to handle and diffuse difficult situations. He said that injury and even death can be daily accoutrements to the job.

It had been agreed on all sides that the teenager had been injured, as well as the officer, in a scuffle which occurred in the car.

The teenager was fleeing and was unarmed.

The speaker said that once the teenager was more than ten feet away and unarmed there was no reason for the officer to shoot him. He said that he could have wounded the teenager.

There were reports that the teenager had stopped and raised his hands, as to surrender, when the officer had called out for him to halt.

At that point the officer should have told the teenager to lay on the ground while he called backup. Since the youth had stopped to comply with the officer's demands there was no more need for violence.

By shooting to kill the officer neglected proper procedure. Had the teenager come back towards the officer, at that distance, he could have wounded him. By killing the teenager he took justice into his own hands and he was responsible for all the protest. He continued to say that his actions defied the training that officers receive and circumvented any hope at real justice.

Once again there was an uproar of voices. Apparently there was a Police union representative and someone else besides the radio commentator in the studio.

They broke for some other callers who called names and espoused violent and disturbing theories.

The commentator allowed the first speaker to continue after some of the name calling became extremely racist.

There was a shout which said that the officer was on the spot and his judgment was the only one that counted.

The caller continued by saying that the training received by police officers do not condone illegal use of firearms and since the teenager was unarmed that the officers use of his authority was flawed. He continued by saying that this was the reason for investigations by internal affairs.

The union representative said that the officer would be found innocent of any wrong doing, at which point, the caller said that it would be a whitewash acquittal since the officer killed the teenager and denied him a chance to plea his case.

As a matter of fact, said the caller, if the officer was as competent as you say, why couldn't he have wounded the teenager? Isn't he trained to and graded on firearm accuracy? Isn't he trained in hand to hand combat?

There were a lot of flustered voices and no real response to the callers accusations.

Then the caller said that the system was failing to represent and protect the people of Ferguson because their response to the killing of the teenager was a militarily armed force to address, confront, harass and intimidate legal protest.

At that point it appeared that the caller was disconnected and the gentleman in the studio were talking about the gathering of looters vandalizing the community.

Tommy said out loud, "One thing lead to another, both were wrong"! That was when there was a knock at the door. Denise was back.

Denise was dressed differently. She wore a tight pair of jeans, a warm gray blouse with a wide collar and a jean jacket with a cotton lining and a hood. She pulled a small suitcase behind her and she carried a duffel bag in her left hand.

She walked into the room and Tommy could sense something different in her.

"What the hell are you listening to"? she spouted. The people on the radio were now openly mocking the caller and telling poor oft-color jokes.

"Yea", said Tommy as he switched it off and attempted to find the sports channel on the television. "My curious brain, Tommy continued, wanted to hear what people are saying and where this crap is going."

Denise laughed. "You guys are funny, trying to solve our problems. What do you care what happens to niggers out here? I know you've got your own problems back East."

"Your problems are OUR problems, replied Tommy. Your misery is my misery. We have to attack our problems together to end them here and everywhere else."

Denise had a look on her face like "so what"?

"We're only niggers if we say so, continued Tommy, what they say about us doesn't matter. Our strength lies in believing in ourselves and making others respect our rights and our presence here."

"Shit, she said, this ain't our country, White folks will tell you that and you see they do what they want."

"My Great Grandparents were born in this country, replied Tommy, I have more rights to call it my country than the whites whose grandparents immigrated here in the beginning of last century. Blacks didn't start immigrating here until way after slavery and then not ......"

Tommy could see that she was neither listening or interested in his opinion or knowledge. The rose had bloomed and was now withering away.
There was a look of distress on her face.

Tommy picked up a joint off the table and lit it.
He handed it to her.
She was sitting on the edge of the bed with a far away look in her eyes. This was how she had looked when they met.
He wondered if he would ever see the woman that shared his bed last night. It seemed that he would never see her again.

Tommy picked up a bottle of beer and opened it.

"I heard that the weather should be clearing up soon", said Denise. She seemed a little looser than when she had entered.
She passed the joint to Tommy.
Tommy took the joint and took a big draw of the smoke into his lungs. He coughed a little.

"I really want to thank you for this ride, continued Denise. It will save me some money for my trip back home. We could get there by eleven or twelve tonight. That would be great because than I can get home quicker".

"Is there anyone there waiting for you"? asked Tommy.

"Well, said Denise, I have a daughter, her name is Jazmine. She is twelve years old. I let her stay with her girlfriend for a few days. They go to the same school. We live in the same apartment building. I also have to return to work. Its hard enough to exist on what I make so I can't miss many days."

Tommy passed the lit joint back to Denise.

He stared at some of the football highlights on the television screen. Had he been home he would have been more interested but at that moment he was feeling some strange vibes.

He stared at the screen while Denise finished the joint and continued to talk about her daughter.

Tommy could hear her but he was distracted by the strange vibes which were bouncing off the walls.

He closed his eyes, maybe it was the marijuana or the changes the trip played on his daily routine/diet. Listening to her talk brought questions to his mind. He heard her words but for some reason he sensed that she was lying.

Tommy opened his eyes. She looked more relaxed but still tense.

Maybe he was wrong. Maybe there was nothing wrong with her and it was all the extra narcotics in his system.

He was still pretty agitated by the dialogue he had heard on the radio.

Denise was right about that. There was nothing that he could do about how these people were going to resolve the tragedy that was gripping the area.

Tommy tried to relax.

She talked about missing her daughter and being ready to return home. She implied that her visit back to St. Louis was a mistake and that it would be her last visit.

She talked about how hard it was on her job as a cashier, how unreasonable the supervisors were and how low were the wages she received.

There was a somber and tearful mood to her.

Tommy could see the tears slowly run down her cheek. The sound of her voice was as if she was under water.

He decided to collect his belongings from around the room. He now wanted to leave as soon as possible. The likelihood of another love fest was very remote.

"As soon as I......(she paused)...As soon as I do this one thing hopefully I'll be able to make some headway in my finances. I want Jazmine's life to be better than mine."

Tommy's mind started racing. What was the one thing she had to do? Why did she come here anyway?

It was like he was seeing her under a new light. The morning light of reason. He could now see the wrinkles and stress lines in her face and her hands. Whatever he had seen in her eyes before was gone and all that was left were two very dark brown beady lumps of coal. The warmth that they shared, he thought, must have been all she had. Maybe it was the high octane of their narcotic filled night. Whatever it had been, he did not see it now.

"So why are you going to Oklahoma City"? asked Tommy.

There was the sense that he surprised her with his question. Her answer was even more odd because her voice changed tonally and she whispered or more like muttered that she had to meet someone and pay off a debt.

"People don't use checks today.", Tommy said whimsically.

Denise seemed paranoid and a little annoyed.

"yeah, I don't know" she replied curtly.

Tommy could see that the rain had ceased beating the window and a glimmer of sunshine was poking through the clouds.

He pulled some meat off the chicken on the table and placed it between a roll. He ate quietly.

This was awkward.

She sat at the table. Her eyes looked so sad and almost petrified. Her present verbal communication was abrupt and ragged.

She talked almost unconsciously and did not respond well.

This was a disaster.

This was another area where Gene was excellent.

He wouldn't care about her problems and he would have had her either in the bed or out the door.

She had already thanked him for the ride several times during her dialogue about her daughter and her life. He wanted to fulfill his promise and continue on his journey.

She reached over and pulled the leg off the chicken.

Tommy handed her one of the two beers left. Quietly she chewed and drank. She got up and adjusted the radio channel to some contemporary hip hop music and then sat back down and continued to eat her food.

The sunlight now was beaming into the room.

Once again an odd feeling came over Tommy. The bright sunlight usually lifts spirits but Tommy felt like he was standing in the shade. Was it the gloomy, tearful, far removed presence of the woman in the room with him. Was it his diet of alcohol, drugs and hastily eaten meals.

He had to admit that he was acting differently and maybe that was where the feeling came from.

He looked at Denise. She was busy chewing and she gave a half hearted smile when she noticed him looking at her.

Maybe she had taken some other drugs when she left. Maybe that what's different/ wrong with her, he thought.

The rain had stopped, the sun was bright and the clouds were moving away. It was time to go.

10

A S A YOUNG man Tommy had once been in jail.
Due to the overzealous and racist Philadelphia Judicial system, he had been charged with assaulting a police officer (in a Police station while surrounded by a room full of detectives).

The charges were thrown out. He hadn't done anything except ask some questions before he was being plummeted by nightsticks and fists.

Regardless, he had to retain a lawyer, miss days of work and suffer the reality that the officers, although in the wrong, would keep their jobs. Meanwhile he had to pay to have his court files expunged. Pay for his legal defense, the doctor and hospital bills he incurred from the assault.

They had placed him in a dark, unventilated holding area after they beat him. It was a room with concrete walls and a steel door. There was a glass square covered by a shutter which the detectives would open to verbally assault those inside.

There were others in this dark area, sitting on the floor against the wall. Tommy only got a quick glimpse. He navigated in this sweaty odoriferous dark environment and found himself a safe area along the wall.

He remembered that someone was whimpering, someone was cussing at the police and another voice was telling jokes.

In that dark room, Tommy's mind was racing. He was totally innocent of any crime but there he was incarcerated and suffering indignities. He didn't know what to expect. There had been one or two black officers in the room when they assaulted him.

The mentality to treat all Blacks as crash dummies was evident back then and with the reports from New York, California, Louisiana, Chicago and other states, the trend had not stopped.

Tommy's mind was racing once again because he found himself in a similar situation.

He sat up on the wooden cot/bench in the detention cell.
The walls were filled with graffiti and chipped, peeling paint.
There was pain in his head from an injury he had suffered.
His arm and back were aching. There were bruises which had been medically attended to but still hurt.
This was totally bullshit he thought, but unfortunately it was real.

He had been here for over twenty four hours.
He had been interrogated. He had been called a liar, an old criminal and a dumb nigger. He had been threatened with more violence, from police, if I did not tell them what they wanted to hear.
A public defender had come into the room and advised him to cooperate with the police and that his sentence would be reduced.

Straightforwardly and truthfully Tommy told them everything he knew. The officers moaned and groaned, they sneered at him. They laughed in his face and tried to incite him to physical violence. They talked about him, as if he were a dog, and implied that he would be mistreated in prison.
During his stay they fed him sandwiches filled with cheese and small juice boxes.
Memories of his youth and the harassment, intimidation and racism which were the tools of the Police continued to flood his mind.
He overheard one of the officers talking about his compatriots in the Illinois State militia (the Sons of Illinois) and how they could make him confess.
Tommy retreated within and blocked out the anger, lies and ignorance threatening his life.
His self taught study of eastern philosophies and meditation quieted his mind.
The years of growing up in a very religious Baptist family gave him the hope and faith that he would survive it all.
Hours of interrogation and times of complete silence gave him the information he needed. The Police tried very hard not to answer his questions but he learned from theirs.

Denise had a record of petty theft, drugs and one of the officers kept asserting Prostitution.

She was associated with Randolph Schultz known in the streets as Randy the Brain.

Randolph was a white guy of approximately thirty some years. He was about six foot two and two hundred sixty pounds of vicious savagery. Randy was identified as a bank thief who had been part of a three man team that robbed banks in some of the surrounding counties. The officers mentioned areas such as Webster Groves, Boulevard Heights, Fenton and Chesterfield.

They were trying to tie Tommy to some illegal activities in those areas.

Tommy was completely ignorant of any of the locations or people they talked about.

Of course he had an acquaintance with Denise and he made been fighting Randy when the Police surrounded them and beat him to the ground.

It all came about because Denise had suggested that there was a great bar/restaurant on their route where they could get some fantastic chicken wings to travel with.

Somewhere outside of a town or area designated as Eureka they pulled into a parking lot to purchase the food.

A big white guy ran up onto Tommy, pushing him and trying to rip his car keys from his hand.

When Randy pulled a huge blade from his belt and advanced towards Tommy, Denise shouted.

"No!!, she said, you promised not to hurt him!

Just give him your keys"!! she shouted to Tommy.

Tommy was scared. He was in a foreign area, confronted by a heavier, younger opponent. Denise had set him up.

He had been raised during a time in Philadelphia were gangs were a part of the urban landscape. It was a troubling period of life when thugs were claiming territory and exacting punishment on those that passed through.

Tommy had come through those times and even if he was neither a gang member or a violent person, he learned a few things.

When Randy advanced on him he timed it perfectly and thrust his right foot into Randy's knee.

Randy buckled and cursed out loud. Tommy had hurt him bad.

Tommy circled around Randy and unloaded a powerful punch to the side of his face.

Randy responded by swinging the huge blade wildly connecting with Tommy's arm.

Tommy remembers going for the knife. He was twisting Randy's arm when he was hit by a branch wielded by Denise.

Suddenly the Police were there and even though Tommy tried to back up, with his hands raised...he was ordered to the ground and hit a couple of times with a blackjack.

At that time Tommy, Randy and Denise were taken into custody.

The car was searched and it was discovered that the duffel bag which Denise carried was filled with money. Money which was identified as coming from one or two of the bank robberies where Randy was seen in participation.

Apparently the Police had been following Randy hoping to recover the money and to apprehend his associates.

The Police had tried to assert that Tommy had been one of Randy's associates.

The idea in one detectives mind was that the fight was brought on because Tommy and Denise had been running away with the money cutting Randy out.

The Police knew that Randy had two associates, both were black.

They were not facially identified because they wore masks. Randy's mask had come off in one of the robberies and the tattoo of the a naked female torso on his left arm was seen in another.

There had been a lot of accusations thrown around.

Even though they thought that Randy's two accomplice were men the detectives seemed bent on making Tommy and Denise fit the bill. There had been nerve shattering shouting going on in the sessions with Tommy.

Apparently the thought was that they could browbeat a confession out of anyone. The threats were their weapon of choice.

Tommy stuck to the truth. He had no other recourse.

Whether or not the Police were doing their job all Tommy could sense and see was that they were hard pressed to make their assumptions correct.

Even though he plead his innocence over and over, the prevailing assumption was that he was lying. By the indignities thrown at him, Tommy felt the lack of respect for Black people in general. He could tell that the officers were under pressure to make arrests and it appeared that the truth only complicated their approval and completion records.

He had to remain quiet much of the time because the officers ignored his words as if they were a contagion.

He absorbed the insults with a casual manner which infuriated the investigators.

Back and forth from his detention cell to the interrogation room.

It was getting ridiculous. Tommy knew that they couldn't prove he did anything. He was starting to get an attitude.

This time when they sat him in the room and he sat awaiting the detective, he was surprised when Denise walked into the room and sat down.

She had been crying and her hair was tossed to hell.

She saw Tommy and immediately hung her head and continued crying.

Tommy looked over at the Observation window and the cameras mounted on the wall. He was leery that she was here to somehow implicate him in some lie.

Tommy placed his arms on the table which sat before him. He sat on one side and Denise on the other.

He groaned slightly feeling the pain from the knife wound on his arm.

"I'm sorry, she said. I told him not to hurt you. You should have just handed him your keys, I never meant to involve you in all this."

"Give him my keys, Tommy shouted. Fuck you and your Boyfriend. I was doing you a favor by giving you a ride to Oklahoma city…. or was that a lie too."

"No…NO!!! (she started sobbing again). I was supposed to meet him there with the money. I needed the money…he never sends any money for me or his daughter."

"Bullshit, said Tommy. You took me to that secluded little bar to carjack me."!!!!

"I'm sorry…I'm sorry, all he wanted was the car to get away. He said he wouldn't hurt you. Now my daughter is without me or that money…we need the money." (she started crying again, this time even louder).

"That is not my fault. You chose that big ass criminal. You are your daughter's mother. Why me??? Why put me into your plans? Did I mistreat you? Why didn't you tell me about your bullshit"?
"I couldn't, she said, still crying. If I had said anything you would have said no or spoiled the plan. Randy would have killed you and took your keys. I saved your life. I told the police what really happened."

"look around, said Tommy. You saved me for this? I have bruises all over. I've been threatened with violence by Police who seem intent on beating a confession out of me and I don't know you or that white faggot ass boyfriend of yours. Bitch!!! Why didn't you leave me alone"?

"That's not what you were saying the other night when you were all up in my space."

"Bullshit!!!, shouted Tommy. I don't deserve this."

"You don't know how bad things are here. You and your Buddy coming here, talking shit!!! Why do you care about these niggaz out here. We do what we have to do."

"Dumb Bitch, said Tommy. Why do I care? it's a matter of justice… Injustice for you translates into injustice for me. If they can justify killing an unarmed teenager thirty feet away, they can justify killing without a reason at all!!!!
Yea!!!! I care about that!

You should have stayed with your daughter. You put yourself into this situation. You knew he was a no good motherfucker when you left. You should not have come back!"

Suddenly the door opened and two detectives came rushing in.

Denise and Tommy were taken back to their separate detention cells.

Tommy sat in his cell thinking.
He was surprised that she did not try to implicate him in her crimes. He had developed an extremely poor level of confidence in her.

Her best option was to tell the truth. Maybe she understood that. There was sincerity when she spoke of her daughter. She loved her and wanted to return to her.

Yea, maybe she was also right about Tommy not knowing how it is for her. She got involved because she needed the money.

Tommy could only imagine that she was working at some minimum wage job trying to raise a daughter and keep the lights on.

Still his blood boiled at the thought that she set him up, endangering his life. Now he was paying for her evil.

He could only imagine that his remarks regarding the Police and the performance of their duties did not make him any other friends behind the observation glass.

The last time he had been within a cell he had to convince people that he did not do anything wrong.

The people at work giggled like he had done something wrong and only gotten a reprieve due to a favorable recommendation from the job and local neighborhood political assistance.

Of course, some of the whites thought it was because he was Black that he received any favorable treatment.

Telling them the truth was funny and bittersweet because they didn't believe him.

This time there would be no one to tell unless the Police charged him or he just decided to tell anyone. Right now there was the real urban fear that they could just take him out and kill him.

The men and women who put on the uniform suffer the highest occupational rates of Divorce, Alcoholism, Drug use, Spousal abuse, civil disobedience violations and abuse to children.

The job is full of pressure and minor injuries are an everyday occurrence. Many on the force are not culturally diverse. Not only do the officers not represent a more diverse makeup but most of the officers have no contact with other cultures outside of their own.

History will prove that white Americans have a very poor record in understanding and respecting other cultures.

It is even evident in their relationship with Americans unlike themselves. They are very unsympathetic with Latino Americans, Chinese Americans, Indian Americans and undeniably African Americans. The fact that members of these other races have been Americans longer than their White counterparts means little in this racist environment.

In this mind frame it is normal to expect one if not more members of the force using their position to inflict pain, use harassment, intimidation and physical force to achieve some personal malevolence outside of their duties on the force.

Regardless Tommy was not going to worry, he thought.

They never charged him and they never would. They would discover that he was who he said he was and that he had never been in the area before.

He had been stupid to have been so trusting of strangers.

He was responsible for that alone.

Tommy sat for another ten hours.

There was no evidence to prove that Tommy was anything more than what he claimed. Although he received the same guilty treatment from the Police Officers when he left.

One of the officers even said to Tommy, "I know you did something and the next time I'm going to take you down"!

They even wanted Tommy to file charges against Denise.
"Why not fry the Bitch"?? That was all they kept saying.

Tommy thought seriously about it for a few minutes.

He looked at the faces trying to get him to indict this woman and keep her from her daughter and a future.

He didn't owe her anything. Randy could have killed him or left him stranded far away from home. She was responsible for that.

"Just sign the papers"!!

He was mad but he found it hard to cooperate with the same people who treated him like trash, whether he was guilty or not.

"They didn't succeed, said Tommy. I have my car. I am just going to leave it at that."

The Police turned belligerent again. They talked about how they could impound his car to search it further.

They even talked about charging me as an accomplice.

The Police Captain nor the local prosecutor would authorize that course of action because they had already compiled his personal and criminal records and there was nothing.

He was given a cold good bye as if he had spoiled their day.

Dragging his body, still feeling the aches and pains of his encounter and jail time, Tommy got into his car.

It was turning dusk and Tommy was tired, but he wanted to get out of the state and far away from these police.

The navigation system pointed Tommy ahead towards Oklahoma City.

11

*O*KLAHOMA CITY IS *a fantastic city. It is a shining example of urban renewal and rejuvenation.*
Driving into the city was like a breath of fresh air and sunshine.
Tommy straightened up.
The pain was still in his bones from his encounter in Illinois.
The majestic calmness of the wide open spaces and the large buildings was a pleasing ecstatic sight.
This was the place to recover.

Oklahoma City was a seven hour drive from St. Louis.
There was way too much time thinking to the sounds of the radio.
Tommy had made two very short stops, both times merely to relieve himself and to pickup snacks and something to drink.
The stiffness in his bones from his bruises and his stay on a wooden bench made him walk more like a man of his senior years.

There were two telephone calls which helped him breakup the solitary journey.

He had only gone, maybe five miles from the police department before he tried to contact Gene.
He had refused to contact anyone during his imprisonment.
Tommy had a certain understanding of Gene and he felt that he would not be taken as he had been. Gene had a command of situations which made him the aggressor. If Judy had any nefarious plans for Gene, Tommy felt, Gene's over the top personality would make her reconsider those thoughts.

Then again, Tommy was nervous that had Gene known where he was that he would have come to the Police Department causing an uproar.

The weapons in the car that he would be driving could only make matters worst.

An hour or so after Tommy had tried to contact Gene, Gene returned the call.

"Damn Man!!!!, where you been? I've been trying to reach you for two days.

I hope that you are not still stuck up in that snatch!!

Man have I got some shit for you."

"What happened Man? You alright? I hope that you didn't get caught up with those weapons"!!

"Whoa, replied Gene. You know I take of business.

That Judy takes me to a set over some dudes house. We were getting down strong. He had some monster product and since we were also drinking, we were acting like some 'class A' fools.

I kept saying we should leave because I was getting as hot as cheese on the grill. She said that she wanted to wait because someone was supposed to meet her there and give her some money."

Tommy could hear loud music in the background and the muffled sound of voices talking.

Gene continued talking.

"So we stay there a while. There were other people there partying and I met a beauty named Jiggy.

I believe they called her that because her movements were fluid and damn sexy.

I was getting ready to pull this babe from this set and take her back to the hotel room. All of a sudden Judy returns, after circulating around with some of her other friends, and she was accompanied by two sour looking brothers.

The dudes looked like bad news.

GARRY JOHNSON

These dudes were pissed, it was written all over their faces that someone had done something to them and they were out for blood.

They asked Judy, "Is this the guy"?
She shook her head and started to introduce them to me.
Can you believe that they were known as Tricky and Jam.

They started right in asking me about you and that Denise.

Apparently Denise was hooked up with some dude called Brain.
Brain took some money from them and they were sure he gave the money to Denise.

They wanted me to contact you so they could catch up with Denise."

Gene started laughing and cussing. Then Tommy heard him order a drink.

"So you know, continued Gene, that I was not going to give them anything. I did not like the way they broke into my groove and I could see that the others were intimidated by their looming presence in the midst of our high times.
I was trying to get with Jiggy.
I told them that I would try to catch up with you later and when I talked to you that I would let you know what they wanted.
(Gene started laughing again)
They wanted me to call you right then. I refused.
In fact I told them to Go Fuck Themselves!!!!
They didn't like it.
(Now Gene seemed to take a breath and he began talking fast)
Man…I was tore up. I was so wasted I didn't give a fuck!!!!
Man.. The dude named Jam was about three hundred pounds and he stood around six feet five inches.
He reached down and picked me up from the chair I was in.
He had massively fat hands. Thick fingers.
He hoisted me up by grabbing each side of my chest. Raising me up where I was looking down on him.

Tricky, was a more stout individual because he stood about five feet tall and weighed close to three hundred pounds himself.

I was so high that I was shocked. The way he picked me up was freaking awesome. I was speechless.

That's when Tricky pulled out a large blade. It could have been a machete.

He started some old weak shit about what he was going to do to me to make me call.

That was probably when I collected my senses and acted."

"What in the hell"!!! Tommy broke his silence.

"What a minute, said Gene. You have heard nothing yet.

Man, I swung my left leg and drove by toe dead into the big fool's nuts. He wobbled and dropped me.

Now I could feel that Jam had a weapon in his jacket pocket.

My right foot had kicked his jacket pocket when he was holding me up in the air.

When he dropped me I picked his pocket and removed his gun.

I fumbled with it trying to grip it.

Tricky raised his blade to swing at me. I pulled the trigger on the gun and fired a shot that went wild.

The firing of the gun may everybody run to get outside.

Jam started swinging his huge arms at me.

He knocked me to the other side of the room with one blow.

Jam came towards me and I fired the gun again. This time I shot Jam in his leg.

Jam's punch had knocked me into a card table and the folding chairs around it. I was kinda upside down having landed on my head and shoulders.

Tricky started coming towards me as I was trying to stand up.

I shot him man! I put a bullet in his hip.

Jam was crying like a little baby. He was grabbing his knee as if he couldn't walk.

Tricky was blown back against a wall and either the bullet or the impact hitting the wall with his head knocked him out.

(Gene started laughing again)
Man I ran out of there, jumped in the car, checked out of the hotel and drove back here before anyone sent the cops my way!!!!
(Gene was still laughing)
Now ain't that some shit!!!!"

Tommy started laughing. The laughter gave his achy body some life. He listened as Gene told him that he was so spooked that he stopped at an overnight parcel service and shipped the case with the Guns, Rifles and Knives ahead.

He said that he tried to contact Tommy continuously for a day or so.

"I knew you could handle yourself, said Gene to Tommy, I just wanted to warn you in case you were still with that bitch."

The two men spoke for close to two hours.

After hearing of Gene's adventure it was easy for Tommy to communicate about his own experience.

The men talked and laughed as if they had front row seats at a comedy club. It was amazing how they could be so casual after having both experienced violent and traumatic situations.

Tommy thought back to his father.
He had been born in 1915 and had seen many things change by the time he died in 1988.
Tommy remembers how he would talk about the cruelty and ignorance of the past. Life was tougher then because many of the modern conveniences that are taken for granted now required man power to accomplish back then.
Transportation, Communications, the general levels of civility that exist now are all different from back then.

Black People took constant abuse. It was in the way they were portrayed in the news, it was prevalent in the housing areas they were restricted to and the available service they had within their neighborhoods.

Tommy's dad used to say that throughout it all that it was hard to break the spirit of Black folks.

Their lives had been full of so much sorry and bitterness. Every time Blacks progressed the White power structure would device another way to push them back or down.

Today there is still voter manipulation and gerrymandering in voting districts. More people of color are receiving High School diplomas and graduating College yet our unemployment rates are still high. Discrimination and racial profiling is still prevalent in hiring and promotions. Funds designated to create, promote and encourage urban revitalization often find their way to other projects.

Blacks are demonized in criminal justice and judicial circles.

Blacks suffer numerous and often verdicts of injustice.

Blacks are killed while unarmed and/or legally protesting for their rights. Blacks have been killed for just being Black in America.

The President of the United States is a Black man and despite his extraordinary performance of inheriting office when it was at a record low, despite the fact that the opposing political party pledged constant opposition and destruction of the presidency, despite the fact that he was reelected and has restored the economy, reduced the national deficit, created a record number of new jobs, despite the fact that Wall street and the business community are experiencing record highs, despite it all there are those who would rate his performance poorly.

Yet, through it all, there are pictures of the president as a happy well adjusted person, a loving father and husband.

He like Tommy and Gene have found a way to laugh through the ignorance and danger.

Tommy's dad was right, he thought.

Blacks are going to live throughout the hardest, coldest and cruelest situations. We would not only survive but grow.

We would laugh through the beatings and indignities.

GARRY JOHNSON

Once you acknowledge the truth, face your enemies and faults there is nothing that can challenge your soul.

The Souls of Black Folks are free.

The conversation was soothing. The company made the drive pleasurable. Navigation kept Tommy going in the right direction and Gene's voice and friendship kept Tommy awake and alert.

There was another telephone call that Tommy had to make.

He dreaded the thought.

He kept Gene on the telephone.

Gene was in a bar/restaurant.

He could hear all of Gene's discussions there and he knew by the liquor requests he could hear and the sound of Gene's voice when it was time to end the connection.

It had been over a week since Tommy had spoken to Tiffany or Eloise.

He had planned to have contacted them by now. The past forty-eight hours left him less than presentable in his eyes and he did not want to talk about or explain those hours to his wife.

Whereas the conversation with Gene had been raucous and full of laughter he knew his conversation with his family was going to be basically serious, very judgmental and full of opinions.

It was kind of funny that knowing this he was still headed for a face to face showdown.

He tried to convince himself that he should call later.

He had all the numbers. Eloise's cell. Tiffany's cell and the house number. He could call the house once Tiffany returned from work possibly catching them both at once.

He was starting to get tired. The pain in his joints was a nagging problem. He knew once he got into a hotel room he would be asleep in little time.

He played the Motown and sixties oldies on the radio.

He would have liked to play the jazz channel but he knew it would relax him too much. He needed to sing and feel the energy of dancing. Much of the Jazz he liked was blues inflected, very soothing and excellent for being alone with your thoughts.

He needed to hear singers singing alongside him.

He had been playing the Funky groove network but the beats made him move his limbs too much.

The Oldies gave him the perfect feeling of dancing without the constant foot patting.

Singing many of the songs gave him energy and inspiration.

It was in those songs that he loved Eloise.

They shared these songs of their youth, even though, they were not together during those times.

Yes it was true that he had known her back then.

Eloise, like so many other young black women, was interested more in their security than in love.

While the guys were gathered around to find love she was searching for Mr. Right. It was difficult back then because the prospects of most Black boys living into men was slim.

The system was racist and dangerous. There was widespread discrimination in employment which meant the prospects of finding a good job, making good money was marginal.

During their youth there was the Black Power movement to address all the injustices but the harder Blacks protested the harder Whites fought back.

Sure White youths were also protesting but they did not have to return to a neighborhood where Police corruption and unfair treatment was the normal. The same type of harassment and intimidation existed then as today. Blacks were jailed at a higher rate, whether they committed a crime or not. Being Black in America was more deadly back then because the system was making political prisoners of those that spoke out.

They were brutally mistreated by the Police and in the courts.

White Americans also did not suffer, as Blacks did, in promotions/upgrades in their finances. Redlining was the normal in housing. Car financing was extremely costly (unfair) for black consumers.

Throughout it all, Black people achieved and progressed despite the legislated foot and cultural backlash.

The songs which Tommy was singing filled his heart with pride and wonder. He had weathered many an emotional social trauma through this music.

GARRY JOHNSON

In many ways he blamed the music for his present frame of mind.

It was in that music that he fell in love with love.

It spoke of endless love and a love you could depend on.

It made him cry and try harder to please those he loved. It made him want to climb the highest mountain and swim the deepest sea.

In the music he learned to cope with the blues of life, living in a world of contradictions and liars.

He was emboldened by the Jazz, Rhythm and Blues and folk singers who spoke of being human, loving, living and honoring the precious gift given by God.

Throughout all the bad moments he remembered the cool jerk, Mickey's Monkey, the Cha-Cha, the slide, The Bop and the Madison. He had Twisted and slow danced to so many of his favorite tunes.

The basement parties with red lights, spiked punch and sweaty encounters were memories that would last a lifetime.

When Tommy and Eloise finally got together, they had both reached a maturity, which at first, allowed them a wondrous love. They enjoyed each others company and shared so many of the same thoughts.

Before the birth of Tiffany they enjoyed trips together on the eastern seashore, taking in concerts, tours of cities and museums, dining at expensive restaurants all while making fifteen cents stretch to cover a dollar and a half of expenses.

Curtis Mayfield was singing "I'm a fool for ya"".

Tommy knew the feeling.

There was no greater joy than caring for Tiffany and Eloise.

He did his best, everything wasn't perfect but he tried really hard.

They inspired him to go to work and endure the crap that existed as the norm back then.

When Tiffany finished college it was as if everyday he could sing, "How we got over".

The music that was playing reminded him of those sacrifices and of the joy and unadulterated happiness he felt for his family.

Unfortunately, something went wrong in his relationship with Eloise.

He had moaned and groaned about it daily. He had come to terms with it, reluctantly.

When Eloise left to visit Tiffany he found it a welcome reprieve from the constant nagging, suspicion and anger that his marriage had become.

He had tried to work things out but Eloise was persistent and Tommy was learning to ignore her.

The whole thing troubled him and he didn't like it but despite his efforts he didn't see it changing.

Now here he was procrastinating instead of placing the telephone call he felt obligated to make.

He thought it over in his head. Why was he making this trip?

He could picture the look of disgust and anger which Eloise had been presenting to him for over the last several years.

He remembered that she had possessed such a beautiful and appealing face. He used to smile whenever he saw her.

He was now hesitant about hearing her voice.

Was he afraid of speaking with her?

He was more afraid at how the conversation would make him feel.

He was afraid that like so many of their conversations that it would end in anger and shouting.

############

THE SUN WAS bright and shining through the large hotel window. Tommy rolled around in his sleep, yet another night of elaborate dreams filled with love, great wonder and danger.

The past three nights were all the same.
He awoke each morning with a feeling of mystery and confusion.
He could never remember the entire dream only bits and pieces. Whether what he did remember was from the dreams, the conversations he had with his wife and daughter or if they were just projections from his ever present thoughts he was not sure.

The past two days he had awoken hazily and ventured out into the city to taste the cuisine and see the sights.
He had seen Saint Joseph's cathedral from afar.
He also saw the new Chesapeake Energy arena and the Chickasaw Brick town ballpark.
He spent a lot of time at the National Cowboy and Western Heritage Museum.

Tommy was fascinated by the displays and exhibits but he also wanted to see the exhibits concerning the African American Settlers and the Black cowboys who contributed so much to the western landscape.
Unfortunately there was not that much to see.
On record there were books and a few videotapes which the museum offered but not much.
Tommy was disappointed but use to the situation.

He discovered that there was a National museum of Black cowboys and Western culture in Fort Worth, Texas.

The fact that so much was not covered about the Black or Chinese Americans who came, settled and contributed to the history and majesty of the American west was/is common.

A racist trend is prevalent in this country.

America is not the product of one race. Although through the racist laws and discriminatory conditions allowed by the government, one race has been able to wrest control of much of the banking, manufacturing and other means of commerce.

Still throughout it all, citizens of color have supported, advanced and contributed to the growth, wealth and development of the country.

Yet, these citizens are underrepresented in many of the history books and National Museums of the country.

It is a sin and injustice that singular museums are the sole repositories of the knowledge and achievements of these Americans.

Tommy carried on, non the less. He was taught that he was obligated to learn everything. The omissions of the museum were typical of the system he had been raised in.

He had learned long ago that he was being selectively taught and lied to. He learned to temper his formal educational by his own inquisitive nature.

Today was no different and like always it was not the only thing on his mind.

Once Tommy had been about an hour or so outside of Oklahoma City, he made the call to his family.

He was tired and needed the conversation to keep him alert.

The pain killers were wearing off. The bumps and bruises he had suffered in his fight and his uncomfortable stay in police custody were exaggerated by his long drive from Illinois to Oklahoma.

There was a stiffness in his joints from sitting behind the wheel and concentrating on the flow of traffic.

He knew that once he got into the hotel he would fall into a deep sleep.

Had Gene been with him he could have slept while Gene drove or he could have bought some more time awake by using cocaine.

GARRY JOHNSON

Conscientiously he knew that having Gene along would have complicated the journey.

Tiffany answered the telephone.
She was happy to hear from her father.
Her joy was uplifting to Tommy. He heard the little girl in her voice that clung to her father. He thought of the baby he rocked, the toddler he played with and the teenager which sought his support and money.

Tiffany totally monopolized the conversation.
She said that there had been some changes at her job. She worked for a legal firm analyzing and even operating business ventures for the firm's clients.
The firm was being taken over and incorporated into a larger firm. The change would mean that she would be released from her duties and would be seeking employment elsewhere.
She informed her father that she had other opportunities and that her severance pay was tremendously generous. She estimated that she could stay out of work for over two years if she chose to.
That's when the tone of the conversation seemed to change.
It was as if she wanted to say something else but was searching for the words.
Then she asked her father how he was and what he was doing.

Tommy paused and took a deep breath. He wanted to tell her without fully telling her everything.
He told her about going to St. Louis with Gene to help him retrieve some keepsakes and other memorabilia that his dying uncle wanted him to have.

Tiffany's tone then became very authoritarian.
"Daddy, Isn't that near all the protests in Ferguson?
Daddy, you don't need to be around that crap. Those people out there are crazy. You didn't go near that, did you"?

She sounded like her mother, Tommy thought.

She told him he was too old to be out there protesting and that he did not have the same concerns as they did. She said that he had money, property and family, that the people out there could handle their own problems.

Tommy stopped her and told her that he was not out there because of the protests, only to help Gene handle his business. He told her that he would never be too old to object and protest against injustice.

Their discussion lasted for about twenty minutes.

"Daddy, please be careful. I have some important I want to talk to you about. As soon as you get home please come out here. I need to talk with you and mom together."

"Is everything okay"? Tommy asked

"I just need you here, she said, now here's mom."

There was a moment of silence.

Tommy took a deep breath, he wanted to sound upbeat, rested and completely calm.

"Hello" said Eloise in a slow, lifeless tone with a bit of attitude.
"Hi" replied Tommy straightening up in his seat behind the wheel.

"So where are You"?

"I am in St. Louis with Gene. He has a dying uncle who wanted him to sign some papers, collect some family memorabilia and a car."

"yeah, said Eloise, who else is with you."?
"Its just me and Gene" replied Tommy.

"I don't buy it, replied Eloise. Why are you there? Why couldn't he do what he had to do alone"?

"Gene asked me to come, replied Tommy. He seemed kind of shaken to see his dying uncle and wanted some company."

"That old ass man, replied Eloise, Did he need to cry on your shoulder? I don't buy it. And what are you doing in St. Louis? Don't you know what's going on there or are you just watching the SyFy channel and those disgusting porno movies at night."?

"Wait a minute", said Tommy. (He took a deep breath).

"And what is wrong with you, continued Eloise, you sound tired.
Hanging out with Gene, are you High or just drunk? I know there are some women around there. You're going to mess around out there and get jailed or worst."

Tommy could hear Tiffany in the background. She was pleading with her mother. "Mom!!!"

Tommy continued to tell Eloise what he could about his trip.
She continued to sound disinterested.
After ten minutes or so of the vague conversation that the two were muddling through, there came another pause.

"So Tiffany asked me to come to California, said Tommy, are you being annoying"?
He could hear her sigh.

"She probably wants you to meet her white boyfriend", replied Eloise.
Once again Tommy could hear Tiffany in the background.
"Please Mom"!!!

Eloise continued, "He is a very nice person, I like him."

"Well, said Tommy, I think I will come there after I get finished here and get back home."

"No need to rush, replied Eloise, we are doing just fine and I don't want to keep you from your boyfriend and whatever bar you spend your nights at."

Once again Tommy could hear Tiffany pleading with her mother.
Suddenly, Tiffany was on the telephone.

"Dad, said Tiffany, come as soon as you can. I really want to talk with you in person."

"Is this about your mother"?

"Mom…well…No! No Daddy. Its not Mom. Please come as soon as you can, I really want to see you."

"Okay" replied Tommy.

"And Daddy, please be careful out there and go home now"!!

That was the end of the conversation but it was still running through Tommy's brain as he walked around the Western Heritage museum.

He had to laugh to himself.
They both questioned why he was in St. Louis and even if they knew he would not be committing a crime….. They feared for his safety.
This is the fear that all Blacks face, law-abiding and criminal, that being black in America will cause unwarranted scrutiny, possibly harm or other unwanted troubles.
You would wonder how Blacks even survive in this environment.
You could imagine that all encounters with the Police would be feared and shunned, after all, to enter a situation repeatedly and expect a different outlook than has been historically established is insane.
Yet that is what happens everyday, People of color, are beset upon by an overzealous police presence who overreact and cause more harm than good……and we continue to hope for a different response.

On the second day of sightseeing Tommy breezed by the Civic center and Music hall, the Myriad Botanical Garden, the Oklahoma City National Memorial and finally the Oklahoma City Zoo and botanical Garden.
He was still convalescing. Old bones and skin with cuts and bruises heal slowly.
At least he had spoken to his family and had bought himself a few more days to get his act together.

GARRY JOHNSON

This is the third day and Tommy had planned to visit the frontier city, the Museum of Osteology and even a shooting sports complex he had read about.

Tommy rose slowly.
The dream occupied his brain or rather the mystery of what had been his dream filled his mind.
He seemed to remember that there were people who had two heads.
He could see their malformations when others couldn't.
He was accompanied by a friend from work, another old sage, with whom he had spent many hours discussing life.
They were trapped in some building with many steps and doors.
He felt betrayed because there was supposed to be some Shanghai-La existence but it was more of a matrix vibe. It was not a dream but reality. He remembered fighting and running. There was blood and chaos.
In addition there was fear in him when he awoke as if the danger still existed.

Tommy had rolled around in the bed until the intensity of the sun on his body finally woke him.
He had left the drapes open so he could watch the sky last night.
A chill ran through him as he tried to piece together the horrifying adrenaline rush which had been his dream/nightmare.

Here he was in another unfamiliar city and he had the freedom to roam. He realized that this departure from his initial plans had not been budgeted but he figured he needed the reprieve to give his body time to heal. He liked to finish new places which presented elements of familiarity.

He had seen the arena and ballpark with the notion of similar facilities in Philadelphia.
He had been to the Mutter Museum in Philadelphia. It had a vast collection of scientific specimens, models, photos and instruments which presented, at the time, innovations in procedures and knowledge. He had picked the Museum of Osteology because of that experience and to gauge the differences.
Philadelphia is the home to many museums and exhibits.

He had a particular interest in exhibits and artifacts which documented the African American experience but that was not his only interest. He had tried to remain well rounded because his father had always expressed that Knowledge was the key to ones salvation.

The visit to the Cowboy and Western heritage museum was rather limited on African American achievements and experiences but because of that visit and his inquiries he did learn of the Cavalry Baptist church in Oklahoma, the Boley historic district and the Attucks school.

He also found that if he expanded his journey and visited Texas that he could visit the Palmito Ranch Battlefield in Brownsville, the Juanita Craft house in Dallas, the Fort Davis national landmark, the Allen chapel African American Methodist Episcopal church in Fort worth, along with the Rutherford B.H Yates house and the Freedman's town national historic district in Houston.

He had not visited the Dred Scott grave site in Missouri but that was because of all the other activities going on back there.

Thinking over what his plans were and what he had already experienced he remembered that their were some women in his dream. Had one of them resembled Denise?

She was right about how he enjoyed her physical company. He had such a fire in his loins.

He knew that was a big part of his problem, he was lonely. He had learned to sit quietly in the company of his own thoughts but his soul was crying out for a mate.

Eloise was his wife. She had given up being his soul mate long ago.

GARRY JOHNSON

13

G *ROWING UP IN Philadelphia is a great experience. There is so much to take advantage of and comfort in.*

Oklahoma city is a beautiful city but it is also a very white town.

In Philadelphia, Tommy was very familiar with the great Caucasian presence but the city is almost fifty percent African American so there was always the comfort of being home.

The experience of living in a city like Philadelphia gave him the opportunity to mingle with other races and find mutual ground.

He was comfortable working with, dealing with and enjoying the company of whites because in Philadelphia he was always aware of his own worth, achievements and failures. There is a presence back home that shows him his value and history when given opportunity.

Now there was also racism and ignorance there.

Wealth and poverty often occupy the same neighborhoods in the city.

White flight to the Northeast region of the city was also accompanied by harsh, inaccurate and mean-spirited words and policies. Philadelphia has its history of racial conflict, Police abuse and troubled neighborhoods where racial mixing is not welcome.

Tommy was still very proud to have been born and raised there.

The Oklahoma papers and news media had covered some very racially charged incidents which only made Tommy feel insulted and disgusted but hardly surprised.

A man suffering some mental collapse, who happened to have been a practicing Muslim, committed a pretty grisly crime. There was an outcry of anti-Islamic rhetoric which was appalling.

A white police officer was being held, awaiting charges, from accusations that he used his authority as a law enforcement officer to rape and have non consensual sex with several African American females. The women had been described as prostitutes, as if that mattered. The last victim of this officers assault was a grandmother, who could not be labeled as a street walker.

Typically, other Caucasians came to the officers defense with insulting and racially charged insinuations directed at the women.

Historically it has been known that women that have been sexually violated are reluctant to report the crimes because the justice system puts them on trial as opposed to putting the rapist on trial.

Anyone can testify that being violated by a thug is probably more humane than by a corrupt cop.

Tommy could only imagine that it took a lot for the women to bring their charges to light. The officer must have been exceptionally demeaning. It was insulting that the women were being treated so unfairly and that racial bigotry was being used as validation by the officer's supporters. Too much smoke not to be a fire was all Tommy could imagine.

Finally there was an Oklahoman resident that found it necessary to paint his truck with anti-Obama and other ignorant slogans.

It amazed Tommy how disrespectful it had become regarding the President of the United States. In a town that hired so many federal employees and housed military personnel it seemed extremely alarming.

He was sure that people have had problems and difficulties accepting the terms of other presidents. The Bush's, Reagan, Clinton, no one liked them all but today bitter, insensitive, ignorant and outright UN-American insults are thrown at the president everyday.

The Congress has lead the way by showing their basic unadulterated contempt for the leader of our country. Despite the fact that the American people voted him in, twice;

Despite the fact that he has helped set the country on a positive tract after the last president left the country suffering a major and unprecedented collapse. The Stock market has never been higher or unemployment lower.

This is the same tactic used by racist throughout the history of Black Americans.

The men and women who volunteered to fight in the revolutionary war, the civil war and even World war two were all treated poorly.

They were discouraged from serving, they were poorly armed and trained. They were given the worst assignments and ridiculed in their performance of their duties.

In every instance they performed admirably and heroically.

They saved lives and furthered the expansion of the country and the goals of the government.

In every occasion they returned home to barbarity from their fellow Americans and the government they served loyally.

They were unprotected from racists, they were hung for protecting themselves after risking their lives to protect this country.

They had to petition to receive the benefits and recognition that was readily afforded their white counterparts.

Tommy remembered how his father had to fight to receive his benefits after serving in World War two and how it took intervention so that they could move into housing they could afford.

Now in the year 2014 after the election of a black president it continues.

The congress has done little except cash their paychecks and receive benefits which they refuse the average American. They have tried to embarrass the president and bankrupt the country hoping to belittle the achievements of a black man who aspired to and succeeded in running this country.

Now there are blatant civil rights violations occurring all over the country by Police officers who are sworn to protect the public and assist in the dispensing of justice.

A young black man can kill a police dog and get twenty three years in jail while unarmed teenagers, innocent sleeping children and even handcuffed black men in police custody are killed without redress.

Many people had thought this was a new era of fairness, justice and understanding but there are forces out there trying to tear it all apart. Its as if the ignorance of the past slave owners is present in the souls of their descendents.

Big money finds it easy to agitate the hatred of the whites they have screwed over by giving them the same opponents they presented before.

After Slavery, Blacks were attacked, burned out, lynched and legislated out of any prosperity; telling the angry white mobs that blacks were taking their jobs.

In spite of those challenges Blacks have progressed.

Graduation from secondary schools and colleges have increased, Employment (even though still lower than whites) is better. The overall economics of Black America have vastly increased.

African Americans are in Politics, CEO's of major companies and Corporations and more visible on International stage and screens.

The Demographics of the country are changing.

That is the reason Tommy believes that so many of the racists are coming out of the woodwork. They feel the pinch. Others are getting larger pieces of the pie.

Although roughly 56% of Oklahoma is white, 15% is African American and 17% is Hispanic. In thirty years through the mingling of the races those numbers will drastically change.

Tommy could see the change every time he traveled across the country. Still some things remained the same because there is another 5.3% of Hispanics who classify themselves as white.

Tommy found all the racial bigotry and ignorance common. He felt that as one man there was little he could do.

He was neither a Politician or a professor.

He just wanted to be treated fairly and unrestricted in his country.

Tommy thought of how similar racial politics was to his marriage. Eloise never listened to him.

Sure he knew there were major differences and above all he knew never to bring that analogy up to her.

Treating him like a white racist was an insult that could get him subject to an endless tirade of invectives to which he could only respond by apologizing.

Tommy had found out some information about the Bizzell library at the university of Oklahoma but he decided to call it a day after he visited the Zoo.

The Museum of Ostelogy in Oklahoma City was more an exhibit of bones than the collection he had seen in the Mutter Museum.

He had wanted to go to the shooting sports complex but he decided that he would save that for later.

He did not own a gun but had tossed the idea around in his head from time to time. Firing a weapon as a sport or skill seemed interesting yet he knew most fired their weapons as practice for shooting another human being.

He also was never a fan of any zoo.

He found the premises funky with the odor of animal feces.

Here in the west people claim to like the smell of the wide open and the manure which is peppered generously across the land to produce growth.

Tommy knew he was just a city boy because to him it just smelled like shit.

Traveling around is an experience by which you might witness new amazing sights, wonderful variations on familiar sights and even the same sight over and over again.

Tommy had the feeling at one point or another that someone was watching him.

He did feel a little out of place. There was nothing western to his attire. He spoke differently and he was constantly twisting his head taking in the landscape, architecture and other sights which many took for granted.

He was aware that there were those that were unaccustomed to seeing Black tourist like him, traveling alone without a mate or family.

He enjoyed his status because he found that many people were pleasantly surprised once they and he talked.

Still he had to be aware of those that might mean him harm.

That was a big city caution which existed everywhere.

He never actually stared into faces but there were some faces which he felt he had seen before.

The dreams which he had been having for the past few nights were possibly crossing over into the daylight.

His stay in Police custody was possibly responsible for the angst he felt. He had been mentally troubled there fantasizing about abuse and even death. Had he actually seen the faces of the officers who had questioned him or was he seeing the similarity in face structure among some of the residents of Oklahoma?

Once in the Western museum and another time when he was having dinner. The image of two heads on one body, two different faces, evil and sinister, staring and growling, always watching him was in his head.

That was probably why he didn't notice his cell phone fall from his pocket. He had dozed off or was just caught up in his thoughts. He somehow noticed a nearby shadow or felt that someone had entered his space when he noticed the boy with his phone.

Reflexes outmatched brain movement.
Tommy patted his pocket and could tell that he had lost his telephone.

Tommy's cell phone was a curious artifact of his possessions.
He rarely used it. He used his telephone in the car more often.
Eloise was constantly complaining to Tommy about his telephone. Did you have it? Was it on?
Eloise would preach that it did not make any sense to have and pay for a telephone that he rarely used or carried.
Tommy countered by saying that the telephone was his possession and not the other way around. He saw it as a safety measure.
There had been times when Tommy had been out at the bar or with friends and he did not hear his phone ringing.
Eloise had gotten to the point where she rarely if ever would call it.
Tommy could write and receive text messages and he had access to the internet but he felt that the keys and the screen were too small.
The telephone was a safety precaution waiting for tragedy.
Regardless, the telephone was his.

The young thief stopped running and ducked into the men's restroom to evaluate his ill gotten game.
The young man was white, fourteen years old, wearing boots and jeans. He resembled thousands of urban black children Tommy was used to seeing.
As he exited the restroom he was greeted by Tommy and a Park security guard.
He started to run, but his path was blocked. He opened his mouth to lie or explain but no words actually came out.

Like most things in life, what followed took time.
Of course the Security guard wanted to ensure that it was Tommy's telephone.
The thief, Travis Rhoades, was a minor without a parent accompanying him.

The telephone calls to alert Travis's parents were unsuccessful.

Tommy was asked to stay around in case charges were going to be filed and the police required his statement.

Tommy sat in the administrative building at opposite ends of a desk from the young thief. The Guard which used the desk left the two sitting there while he was called away for a different situation.

All the time the guard was gone Travis pleaded with Tommy not to press charges. He said that he lived with his dad, who was unemployed, and that he had not eaten for days.

He said that he was sorry but he saw the telephone on the ground and he knew he could get good money for a phone like that.

He fluctuated between crying big crocodile tears and sobbing like he was hurt.

Tommy could tell by his clothes that he must have been sleeping in them. There was a warm spot in his heart for children that lived below the poverty level. He had seen a newscast last night that discussed how 24% of the children under eighteen years old living in the Oklahoma city area lived below the poverty line.

Travis spoke with the vocabulary and nuances of a child who lived on his own.

Tommy knew that Black children who are faced with the same predicament are never treated so humanely but he could not let that sway his personal humanity.

In his eyes this was the case of a poor, dumb kid doing something stupid.

When the security guard returned he once again tried to reach Travis's father. After a couple of attempts he started talking about contacting the Police and handing the boy over. He told Tommy that it would take possibly another hour or two and that Tommy should remain to answer their inquiries.

The day was now wasted and Tommy was hungry and tired.

He wanted to go back to his hotel and sleep.

Against all better judgment Tommy told the officer that he was satisfied that his telephone was back in his possession and that he would not be filing charges if they could end this session and he could leave.

By the time Tommy was leaving the zoo grounds the security officer had released Travis and he also was scurrying to get away from the premises

Once again the goodness of his heart spoke and Tommy, seeing the boy leave, offered to buy him a meal.

Tommy had planned to go to a downtown venue where they treated their fried chicken wings with whiskey. He had been building up a taste for them but he took Travis to a local sandwich shop instead.

Travis did eat like someone who had not eaten for days. He gobbled down his whole sandwich and fries before Tommy could finish half of his meal. He refilled his large soda cup three times before he seemed full.

He thanked Tommy more than once for the meal and not handing him over to the police. He said that his father was a drunk and if he had been arrested that he would get beat bad.

Travis asked Tommy if he wanted to score some drugs. He said that his father used and he knew how and where to get it. He said that he had scored for his dad all the time.

Tommy was now very tired and disgusted.

He thought about giving Travis the speech about drugs.

Tommy only could imagine that the boy's contact would place him in an area and with people who could only be viewed as dangerous.

"No, said Tommy, I don't want anything, and I would advice you to just head home and count your blessings."

"Well, countered Travis, can you please drive me home. It is not far but walking could take a little time. I don't have any money and I better get home. Maybe I can get there before my dad is looking for me."

Tommy thought about it.

He was trying not be ignorant or unkind.

He had been raised in a religious family. He had respect and felt empathy for others whether they afforded the same to him or not.

He felt that this elevated him from racists and morons who populated the world.

He had very little cash on him and he was not going to the ATM machine with Travis in tow.

GARRY JOHNSON

"Okay, Tommy said, as long as its not far. This has been a long day for me and I believe I have shown you more than enough compassion."

Travis was right. It was not that far although when Tommy exited the paved road and traveled down a dirt road he did become rather tense and very cautious.

The house was a one level ranch style building. It had seen better days. It needed paint and it appeared to slope on one side.

The screen door/ storm door was raggedy and did not close. Two of the front windows were cracked and one was boarded up in a patchwork manner.

Tommy pulled around in front of the house.

Travis got out and approached the house. He waved to Tommy and said Thanks.

A man came to the front door as Travis approached.

Tommy figured it was Travis's father.

The man shouted at Travis.

"Where the fuck you been? Is that a Nigger in that car? What have you been doing?!! You got any money."?!

Travis ran up to the door and the man struck him against his head. The boy stumbled sideways.

Tommy watched as Travis ran past his father into the house.

That's when his father shouted at Tommy,

"You better get out of here Nigger before I shoot your ass"!!!

Tommy drove away.

There have been reports of Blacks coming to the assistance of whites and being killed for their efforts.

In the minds of some being black is scary just like the character in "The Green Mile". That type of ignorance is often unchallenged in general white society because they know few blacks personally.

They claim knowledge of blacks from the stereotypes and lies they are fed.

Tommy was not planning on being a statistic.

7+7

A NOTHER NIGHT OF *crazy dreams.*

He was once again in that dark detention room.
People were crowded in the room awaiting charges, sentencing or death he couldn't tell.
They were one by one telling their stories.

A voice said, "I was just going to the store. This dude came up to me and asked for a cigarette. I reached into my pocket and gave him one out of my pack. After he walked away a police officer came up to me and accused me of selling loose smokes. He called me a liar and started pushing me around. I took out my telephone and started to record the encounter. He cussed me out, took my phone and smashed it against the ground. When I get out of here I am going to sue that motherfucker."

Another voice answered, "You ain't getting out of here brother. You're going to die"!

There was laughing. Someone started singing "Swing low, sweet chariot" and the laughing only intensified.

There was loud and joyous sex.
He remembered looking at her face and seeing two faces, one sinister and menacing and the other face was sweet and seductive.

Somehow he was standing with a machete chopping off both heads. Next he was covered with blood from head to toe. He remembered wiping his face and tasting the blood in his mouth.

Another voice in the dark said, "I going to get out of here my brother is a cop."
It was answered by another voice in the dark, "Harold is that you"?

All the time he thought he could hear Eloise saying, "I told you so, you just don't know shit."

And other times he could hear tiffany's voice saying, "Daddy...Daddy.. Daddy"!!!

In between he thought he saw black soldiers swinging from a rope still wearing their uniforms.
There were glimpses of fat rich white men counting money, smoking big cigars while black women and children in dirty, dusty and torn clothing hauling huge bales of cotton to be weighed.

In many parts of the dream he remembered being with his old friend but in waking he always felt he had been alone.
It was strange and eerie, waking in a fearful panic.

Upon waking up Tommy was lethargic.
It appeared to be another clear day with bright sunshine.
The skyscrapers which rose up against the flat Oklahoma landscape presented a picturesque and tranquil vision.

It seemed to Tommy that some of the dreams came out of his life experiences and his quest for historical knowledge. He felt he was being haunted by the past and tortured by the present.
Typical faces in his dreams were never black or white unless they were familiar faces that belonged to someone. These dreams were signs, symbols, road directions from pictures, maps and memories which were in his brain.
Seeing the faces of the Police from Missouri following him were those dreams taking life.

Going through his clothes he had discovered one marijuana cigarette and a small amount of cocaine that he had forgotten.

Once he had decided to leave St. Louis he packed away everything in a haste to drop Denise off and continue on his way.

He never thought about it because they were not a part of his everyday life.

Now noticing that he had them in his possession he wondered if he could use them to calm his mind and ease his physical pain…at least for a short time.

He had already spent more time and money here in Oklahoma than he had planned.

He needed to move on yet he could use a day or so more of just relaxing his aches and bruises.

His only plans for the day were to go to the shooting complex.

He never owned a gun and never really wanted one.

The recent events in the news, all across the nation made him wonder if now wasn't the time to reconsider.

Gun deaths rank high in America. Either you use a gun or someone will use one against you.

Here in the west they fantasize about the old days when men would face each other in the street and one on one shoot it out over politics, women or just too much liquor.

In reality it was more a cowardly shot fired from behind or anywhere not in clear sight. In reality the duels were often lopsided and more a contest of one upsmanship than a contest of skill.

Rarely today are the gun battles that occur about anything more than spraying an area with bullets. Too often criminals, soldiers and even Police hit bystanders and not their targets.

It becomes more common to shoot someone unarmed.

Gun violence is the ultimate bully tactic following only the bombing of an area.

Tommy could remember being a child and hearing of the western shooting legends like Wild Bill Cody and Annie Oakley.

They were stories of dead eye accuracy.

Today Police, even though they train for accuracy, don't shoot for accuracy only to kill.

Swat teams are trained for that one shot…the kill shot.

Even though they also can shoot to disable and maim, the kill shot is the only shot they prefer.

Gene had informed Tommy that he had shot two men in St. Louis.

He had left them both alive. It sounded like he was just lucky to have hit them at all but Tommy was sure that the result suited Gene.

Most black families do not own firearms.

Sure there are more everyday but the possession of firearms in the hood are seen differently than they are in the suburbs.

In the suburbs they may visit a firing range more often than gun owners in the hood. One reason is proximity.

Then gun owners in the suburbs may go hunting in the wild more often, once again because of proximity.

Now it does not reduce the likelihood of death whether you live in the hood or the suburbs.

Gun deaths in American cities are more likely to be murders whereas gun deaths in rural areas are predominantly suicides.

Almost 80% of African Americans favor gun control as opposed to maybe 48% of whites.

The rural areas are more opposed than urban or suburban areas to any form of gun control.

68% of all homicides were weapon offenses and 73% of them were with handguns.

Tommy knew that having a gun often precipitated violence. If you are home and something happens, people go running for their guns. If you are on the street and something occurs to upset, rattle or offend one (and you are armed) the gun is brought out as defensive security.

While working for the city, Tommy met a lot of people.

He heard the story of a Probation officer who carried a gun.

One wintry day in Philadelphia, when a massive storm had hit the city, many employees were trying to get to work.

This guy had volunteered to pick up several people using a city vehicle and bring they into work because the transportation lines were sluggish and some areas were just cut off.

He was making his way into work and because of the weather and the patience of others was involved in a fender bender.

When he got out of his car to discuss, review and exchange information with the other driver, tempers flared and a tussle between he and the other driver pursued.

In that melee, the officers gun was dislodged from its holster.

The other driver seeing the weapon picked it up and fired it at the officer, in his opinion he was claiming self defense.

The officer was injured but no one died.

Tommy always took from that story that if the gun had not been present the situation may never have escalated to deadly proportions.

Then again Tommy knew that gun ownership was another freedom that separated African Americans from White Americans.

The right to own a weapon and defend yourself from threats of life and property are basic. If you want to be seen as the captain of your own ship then gun ownership was purchasing the boat.

Today there are too many semi-automatic and efficient palm sized weapons available. No one needs a semi-automatic gun if you're not in the military and the small guns are just to easy to carry which makes them too readily comfortable to use.

Regardless, Tommy ditched those thoughts and prepared to spend a day indoors watching television and sleeping.

The first thing he did was to venture out to the whiskey wing joint and purchase a large order.

He made sure to get a large salad and lots of fries.

He bought a twelve pack of a good rich, dark imported lager and he checked at the front desk if he was in a room where smoking was permitted.

Of course he did not tell them he was smoking marijuana but he remembered how Gene had secured that information when they were in St. Louis.

The secrecy of the day Tommy was planning made him feel younger. He had felt this way before when he and Gene had gotten together. He imagined the time he could have if he had female company. He laughed to himself because he knew that adding anyone to his day of planned silence, sleep and rest would change what he was trying to accomplish.

GARRY JOHNSON

The news was still upsetting. The protest in Ferguson were now spreading around the country. Other communities and reports of unarmed teenagers and children being killed by local Police were starting to surface. There was crying and shouting.

It was a Fox News station and the narrators and commentators were very bias, uninformed and ignorant. Tommy changed to a local news station. They too were covering the growing protests and even if he found no blatant reason to question their reporting he still felt it lacking empathy.

Tommy propped himself up on the bed using the additional pillows he had requested.

On the bed before him he had spread out some promotional papers from the hotel. He placed his wings and fries in their container on top of the papers. The beer was on the table next to the bed.

He had the Marijuana joint placed in an ashtray next to the beer.

He settled back and starting surfing the channels.

There was a mixed-martial arts fight on.

It grabbed Tommy's interest.

There were two women. It was the last minute of a three minute round.

One combatant in gold trunks with a white stripe, was busy moving around and throwing her feet into the defense of the other combatant who was wearing black and gray.

The fighter in the gold trunks changed her approach and tried to move in on the other fighter with body punches.

The fighter in the black and gray trunks prominently blocked the body blows and then swiftly spun around and landed a blow to the back of the head of her opponent with her fist.

When the fighter in the gold trunks backed away, the other fighter moved in.

The fighter in the gray trunks, kicked her foot high into the air.

The woman in the gold trunks backed up again towards the ropes, then the other fighter lunged forward and connected her knee to her opponents chin.

The fighter in the gold trunks reacted immediately and covered up.

She received a broken nose in the encounter and was bleeding profusely.

The fighter in the gray trunks threw two jabs with her right foot and followed it with a powerful left fist jab which connected.

Automatically the fighter in the gold trunks collapsed. The other fighter was on top of her pounding her head with powerful blows.

The referee separated the fighters because the fight was over.

The fighter in the gold trunks was unconscious and unable to continue.

Tommy changed the channel.

There so many home shopping networks. They were selling computers, sausage and cheese boxes, sweaters, vacuum machines, juicing machines and jewelry.

On the food networks they were discussing mussels, visiting bars and grills in Tennessee, a chef was cooking shrimp with lobster sauce over vegetable basmati rice.

There were several do it yourself channels were they were making repairs in homes and repairs to homes that amounted to minor renovations. There were two wholesale renovations going on, one in Los Angeles, California and another in an upstate New York Mansion out in a farm community.

There were too many movies to choose from.

There were horror movies, dramas, comedies and action films.

Tommy thought that he would like a nice science fiction drama with great special effects, popular actors and an interesting story.

It really didn't matter.

Tommy lit the joint and took a deep drawl. It hit him in a second.

He felt as if he had just stood back and was observing everything with a clearer if not cloudy eye.

He gulped down some beer to quench the dryness he felt.

He changed the channels indiscriminately. It didn't matter his consciousness was in a good place. He was insulated there.

He felt very comfortable and secure. There was no evil here. He could relax. He took another puff.

The television was playing the first Godfather movie.

Tommy had seen the film a half a dozen times.

The chicken wings were delicious. He popped one to another in his mouth and stripped the meat away from the bone with his teeth.

GARRY JOHNSON

He pulled the bone from his mouth and gave it tiny nibbles removing any meat left on the bone. He sucked his fingers and shoved the potato fries through his lips following the chicken.

He repeated the process over and over.

He made a stack of chicken bones in the top of the container of food. The wings were hot, spicy and after having been soaked in whiskey, very intoxicating.

He took a few more puffs to reduce the slight feeling of nausea.

After hearing the music of the wedding party in the movie he longed to hear some jazz.

He could almost hear a saxophone and trombone start out playing.

They played different riffs that met at similar notes which seemed to create a horizon. The Trumpet came heralding out notes announcing a break and a whole new beginning.

As the piano strode across its notes there was a song in his heart which defied words. The piano and the guitar played the melody with great force and skill.

The horns would come back with echo and call, then they would glide across notes leading to the horizon.

A flute would dance through the rhythms and the driving beat which was the base for the rhythm.

The flute and the other horns talked, screamed and sang to each other. Their conversation was intoxicating, hip and lively. The solo by the bass player demonstrated how it grounded ever other note played.

The music translated to kinetic energy which gave a bounce and a sway to the very air.

Tommy could see the sun rising and feel the warmth of security.

The music was riding out a refrain of physical and spiritual seduction.

Tommy existed in that moment of divine peace and satisfaction until we awoke to the ringing of his cell phone.

Tommy had been soundly asleep for almost five hours.

He awoke refreshed, although annoyed by the ringing phone.

He had not experienced any dreams aside from the music that played in his head.

The television was still on and now an action film about a S.W.A.T force was on the screen.

Shaking himself awake Tommy answered his telephone.

Eloise jumped right in.
"Where are you? I have been calling the house for days and you are never there. I took a chance on calling this number. I am surprised you have it with you and its on."

Tommy listened to her monologue until he felt it was actually his turn to answer.
He looked around the room. It was turning to evening. The sun was getting ready to make its exit until tomorrow.
He did not want to tell her that he was camped out in a hotel in Oklahoma City watching an action film which just turned sexy as one of the team has a scene with a couple of prostitutes. He also did not want to talk about his wounds/ bruises or that he was getting wasted.

He sat up in the bed moving the food container further away from him. He took a drink of his beer, which was now warm.

"I hear voices, said Eloise, who is there with you and where exactly are you?"

"That's the television, Tommy turned down the volume, I told you that I was traveling. What's so urgent that you call me complaining and screeching into my ear?

"Not that you would be concerned if I or your daughter had any problems! You are only concerned about that bar, those old cronies and yourself. No!! you don't have time for us!"

At that time Eloise slammed the telephone down breaking the connection. Tommy was stiffly confounded, bewilderment was in his eyes.

He walked in silence to the bathroom. He thought it was the pressure he had to relive. When he came out there was a drum solo marching in his brain.
The telephone had not rung again but he was awaiting on it.
Obviously there was something wrong. He had been here before.

GARRY JOHNSON

Once she had gotten mad it was all over. There would be no reasoning with her.

He retrieved ice to cool the beer he had left.

The telephone did not ring.

Twenty minutes had passed, so he called and she did not answer.

Now Tommy considered lighting up the joint.

What he needed was a bottle of Jack Daniel's.

No! he thought, she would call back and he needed to be in a sober mind.

He decided to take a shower. He needed the warm water running over him to bring him clarity. The phone did not ring.

He took a nice long soapy shower and he felt refreshed when he stepped out.

The warm water felt good on his sore muscles. The bruises were starting to disappear and the cut on his arm was healing well.

He brushed his teeth for an extended period. The mint taste left in his mouth felt refreshing as he sucked down one of the ice cold beers.

He called Eloise. In another ten minutes he called again.

It was starting to irritate him and he was in the dark as to why.

Tommy looked in his telephone and called Tiffany.

"Hello Daddy"

Tiffany had looked at her caller ID before she answered.

"Daddy what are you doing? Where have you been? Mom and I have been calling home. Are you okay?"

"Hello Baby, said Tommy, I am fine. I was just taking care of the business with Gene."

"What did you say to Mommy? No! No!! I don't want to know. I just want you to come here. That's all we wanted. We want to know when you're going to get here."

There was silence for a moment.

"Well we are finished in Illinois and Gene went home earlier.
I decided that I would drive the rest of the way there. So I am in Oklahoma city."

"Daddy are you sure you should be driving that far alone."

"I'm fine. I just scraped my arm helping Gene move something around. As a matter of fact, I have been a little tired so I thought I would stay here for a day. There are approximately eighteen to twenty hours of driving left. Its going to take me another four days. I will stop at the first signs of fatigue and I only plan on driving seven to ten hours a day."

There was silence.

"Daddy you're going to drive the whole way by yourself. I don't know. I don't know."
Tiffany's voice was full of concern.
"Daddy, she continued, why don't you leave your car there and take a plane here"?

"Baby, why would I want to leave my car in Oklahoma City. I'll be fine. Remember, I am a grown man...even your father.. I can handle this."

There was a discussion going on.
Tiffany was talking to her mother.

"So what the hell are you doing"?
Eloise's voice was loud with extensive attitude.
Tommy knew not to feed into it but sometimes he failed.

"I just told Tiffany that I would be there in about four days. I decided to drive across the country. Gene was given a car by his uncle, so instead of returning home to an empty house, I decided to travel across the country and see America."

"Yeah, and who is with you"?

"What is your problem. You left me home alone and you lost your privilege of being jealous a long time ago."!

"What is that supposed to mean? You are still married."

"Words you use to control me, you do not care about me or our marriage."

"O, Hell with you. You can drive your dumb ass in a ditch. I don't care if you come here or not. You're right I don't need to see you.
You can turn around and go home............"

Tiffany was on the telephone.

"Listen you two. (she giggled) Daddy be careful but come straight here. You and Mommy are going to have to stop all that arguing."

There was a lighter conversation. Tiffany was scolding her parents and pleading with her father to be careful. Eloise had already left the conversation.

@#$%^&*15*&^%$#@!

IN THE PAST African Americans were very skeptical and cautious traveling across the country. Even after the end of 'Jim Crow' laws, there existed and exists to this day unfair and overzealous policing of African Americans.

In the past a publication was used by African Americans to navigate their way across the country.

The motorist traveling guide helped Black Americans find places to eat and find lodging.

Tommy was happy that he did not need such a guide today but there were instances where he felt it would be helpful.

The western and rural areas of the country are excellent places for motorcycling. In many of those areas there are motorcycle clubs which have activities which border upon illegal.

Even if they profess to be law-abiding it has been documented that some of these groups perform in manners which could be seen as harassment and intimidation for other occupants of the road.

Tommy had seen many a drinking establishment in his journey that seemed to cater to the motor cycling public.

The trip from Oklahoma City would take Tommy through Amarillo, Texas, Albuquerque, New Mexico, Flagstaff, Arizona and finally into Los Angeles, California.

He did not want to stop.

He had been totally consumed in thought during this leg of the journey. After his conversation with Eloise, he convinced himself that he was accurate in his first thoughts about the trip. Eloise did not want to see him and there was no reason for him to think that they could have any conversation that would not end in an argument.

He had never been able to figure out when it actually started.

One day the arguments were followed by another day of arguments. He remembered that there was a time when they were in love, making love and communicating in soft loving tones. Those days disappeared.

Eloise is a very private and personal individual. She has very few friends and generally displays attitudes of disgust concerning those around her.

Childhood can be a very traumatic experience. Eloise's parents were both dead and she has a very distant relationship with her sister. She has cousins and alike but they are more distant than her sister.

The history of women rights and achievements in the United States is marred by endless tales of abuse, discrimination and ignorance.

It is amazing of some of the positions which women now publicly hold because it has not been so long ago that the doors were closed and expectations were dismal.

Still, the equality of women is not a guaranteed fact in this the country which touts liberty, freedom and justice for all.

This is doubly confounding for women of color who have been working constantly and never receiving the recognition they have earned.

All of this was going through Tommy's brain when he decided to pull over at a roadside watering hole in Texas.

The truth was he did not want to stop but he felt that he should just to give his eyes and mind a relief from those white lines.

Tommy was consumed in his thoughts, he desperately needed to talk to some one if not only for a minute to break the monotonous inner voice.

He pulled off the main highway and into the off highway area of fast food, gasoline, and franchised restaurants. Along with the other establishments was a quaint looking building which advertised delicious sandwiches, cold beer and sports television.

Tommy parked right in front of this building and made his way up the steps.

If Tommy was not still consumed in his thoughts he might have noticed that the parking on the side of the building was consumed by motorcycles.

He climbed the steps which placed him on a landing, a porch, which circled the building.

Had he entered the side entrance he would have also noticed the building name painted across the second level of the establishment. It read 'Confederate Post'.

He pushed the swinging door open and walked into a dimly lit room which was populated by hairy white dudes in leather sleeveless jackets. There was an overbearing smell of beer in the air. The waitresses were outfitted in brief daisy duke shorts.

There was country music blaring and the main object of the song was about an outlaw.

The room was lively. There was an area of three pool tables. Each table had a game going and there appeared to be way more people over there than were involved in the game.

Tommy finally came out of his self imposed inner thoughts to realize were he was.

He stopped for a moment.

He did not what to do next. He had been in many places where he was the only person of color but for some reason this seemed different.

Regardless, he did not want to turn around and walk out so he walked over to the bar and sat down.

Many of the patrons wore bandanas either on their head or around their necks.

The bartender, a huge man of possibly six feet eight inches tall and three hundred pounds of girth, stood in front of Tommy with a face registering genuine disgust.

He did not speak.

Tommy, feeling the oddity of the moment, asked for a bottled beer.

There was loud talking all around the room.

The liveliness of communication enriched Tommy. He had been listening to similar playlists on the radio and his own thoughts for miles.

The bartender came back with Tommy's beer.

Tommy looked up at the television screens around the room.

There was sports news, some talk show and what looked like a high school football game.

GARRY JOHNSON

One of the waitresses came over and asked if Tommy needed a menu.
"Hello darlin', you need a menu"?
She looked at the bartender
"Harold, why didn't you give the man a menu"?
The bartender, Harold, scowled and pulled a menu from under the bar and placed it before Tommy.

After looking over the selections, Tommy ordered a sandwich and some fries.
He sat waiting on his food not knowing if he would be able to eat it. His presence did not seem to offend the general crowd but he felt out of place and that some eyes were definitely on him.
He drank his beer and ordered another.
The conversations around him were numerous. He heard angry voices, shouting, loud laughter and more cussing than he had heard for days.
He was able to relax and melt away into the cacophony of sounds which filled the room.
It was a large place. Tommy could see that there were booths against the far wall but he could not make out much else.
The side door would open and close several times allowing a little more light into the room. The opening and closing of the door also allowed Tommy to see the motorcycles neatly parked in that area.
The music was loud and even though the song had changed several times it always centered around outlaws, women and drinking.
It was amazing how the music was loud enough to have disguised/overshadowed the loud sounds of the motorcycles.
Tommy looked over his food as the bartender sat it before him.
He was wondering if he could trust that it had not be given some extra treatment in the kitchen.

The bar was filling up with patrons. There was a seat separating Tommy from the patron to his right but to his left a group of guys with cowboy hats and boots were discussing someone who they did not like.

Suddenly, the television screen filled up with a local news program. Scenes from the protests in Ferguson and across the nation were shown and discussed.
Tommy could feel the sweat dripping from his underarms.

Once more he felt the eyes of others on him.

The man sitting to Tommy's left became very animated and loud.
"This is bullshit"!! he shouted.
"Fucking motherfuckers"!!! was another echo of voices Tommy could hear behind him.
The room seemed to come alive and Tommy thought they were all focused on the news stories on the screens around the room.
There was shouting and cussing.
Tommy tried to stay within his space but his eyes and the eyes of several of the other patrons met.
The gentleman to Tommy's left stood up and leaned over to Tommy.
"What the fuck do you think"?
It seemed that the whole room became quiet.
In reality it didn't but Tommy could not hear the music or any other voices.
Tommy looked directly into the man's eyes.
This guy was fuming, his eyes were wide and he gritted his teeth.
"What you got to say... Brother"?
Tommy could hear the word brother echo into his very soul.
He had so much he could say. He felt he was in the wrong place to say everything he felt. He looked around the room. He felt alone and at the mercy of wild unruly crowd.
Had this been what others felt before they were lynched, he thought?
The eyes were upon him and he could feel the time passing.
"FUCK THE POLICE"!!!! Tommy shouted.
"Fuck The Motherfucking Police", he shouting again.

There was a moment of silence and awe defying confusion.
Tommy was standing up.
He was waiting for the onslaught of indignities to be shouted at him. He braced himself for the physical onslaught that that might follow.

A howl went up throughout the room.
"Yeah, That's right, said the man to Tommy's left, FUCK THE MOTHERFUCKING POLICE"!!!!!!

GARRY JOHNSON

There was a revived energy in the room. Shouting, Hooting and Hollering.

The waitress came over,
"Darlin', (looking at Tommy's plate) is the food alright"?

"Yeah, replied Tommy, I guess I was not as hungry as I thought."

"Well don't let them get you caught up in their bullshit. One thing for sure they are all a bunch of no good low life country bumpkins and you hit the nail on the head, sugar, there is no love for the Police in here."

Hearing the waitress call him 'sugar' reminded him of being home.
Tommy settled in, sitting straight up on his high bench stool.
He even took a bite of his burger and found it tasty.
The gentleman to his left was named Randy and Randy insisted on buying Tommy a shot of Jack Daniel's and another beer.
Then Randy told Tommy of several run ins he had with the police.
Randy even produced the loaded weapon that he carried in explanation of one of his encounters.

Tommy felt amazingly good.
He had stood up and spoke his mind and even found a sympathetic crowd. He was not sure how far he could express his political beliefs but he was proud that he had stood up for what he believed.

Biggs was a burly guy. He had a lot of facial hair and he worn his hair long down his neck. He was about forty to fifty years old. He explained that he had driven a truck for years but was now experiencing a lull in employment.
A funny thought came into Tommy's head. He wondered if Biggs blamed Obama for his current woes. It was another thought Tommy kept to himself.
Of course they called him Biggs because he was also a local eating champion, his specialty was chicken wings
One story lead to another and Tommy was starting to become bored and antsy.

Biggs may have not been a bad guy but he had a lot of stories about him and the Police.

The crowd in the bar was still lively and the traffic became brisk.

Tommy had been facing Biggs when he noticed a hush go through the room. Biggs stopped and sat up straight, breaking his conversation.

Tommy turned around to see a Texas State ranger walking into the room and walking straight towards him.

"Are you the owner of the dark green Cadillac out front"?

"Yeah, said Tommy, is something wrong with my car."

"I need you out front sir."

Tommy tried to remain calm but he could once again feel the sweat rolling down his skin.

"What is this about officer."

"Sir, I need you to follow me outside...... NOW."!

Tommy could hear the command in the officer's seemly request.

He stood up and started to follow the officer to the front with the eyes of the room on him.

Someone shouted, "Fuck the Police"!!

There was laughter. The officer stopped for a second to survey the room but the darkness prevented him seeing clearly.

Tommy saw the waitress and stopped.

He reached into his pocket to retrieve money to pay his bill.

Randy shouted, "Go ahead brother, I've got the bill."

Outside Tommy noticed that standing next to his car was the officer from Missouri who had threatened to get him.

"What's this all about", requested Tommy.

No one answered him.

The Texas State Ranger spoke to the Missouri detective, "Is this your man"?

"Yeah, replied the detective, I'll take it from here."

Tommy stopped dead in his tracks.

"What's this all about. I have done nothing wrong and this man and I have nothing to discuss."!!!

The Missouri detective walked over to Tommy and shoved him aside. With his back to the Texas Ranger the detective whispered into Tommy ear.

"Look, you bastard. I know that there was about one hundred thousand dollars missing from the money we recovered. That dumb bitch you were with does not have it and that leaves you."
Tommy backed away from the detective.

"Bullshit!!!, I don't have your money, I never met that woman before I got to St. Louis and I don't care what you believe... I have nothing to do with those crimes."!!

The Texas Ranger looked puzzled.

The Missouri detective once again moved closer to Tommy.
"We have picked up Brain's accomplices, they don't have the money. You do!!!! Either you give it to me now or I will take you out of here and beat the truth out of you.... so what's it going to be old player."

Once again Tommy stepped away from the detective.

"This man is crazy. I do not have a record or any knowledge of the bullshit he is trying to lay on me. I am not going anywhere with him."!!!!

As Tommy stepped away the detective withdrew his service revolver and pointed it straight at Tommy.

Unaware to the detective, the Texas Ranger and even Tommy, a crowd of the bar patrons had started to form on the front porch landing of the building.

"Fuck the Police, Fuck the Police, Fuck the Police"!!!!!
The shouts started getting louder and you could hear other voices screaming.
"Stop it!!! he's not doing anything!!!!!"

The Texas Ranger shouted out to the detective, "Stand down, Stand down"!!!
He walked closer to the detective. He repeated his commands as he himself withdrew his revolver.
"Stand down, he repeated his command, you have no jurisdiction here..... we're going to command center and putting this to rest."

Tommy stood with his hands throw up in the air.
He was visibly sweating buckets.

The Texas Ranger walked over to Tommy, placed his hands behind him and cuffed him.

The crowd was chanting, "What are the charges?!..... Bullshit arrest!!!!... FUCK THE POLICE!!!!!"

The Ranger called for backup.
Within minutes several vehicles arrived.
Tommy was once again going to lockup.

The crowd was dispersed and everyone went back into the bar.

GARRY JOHNSON

8+8

*I*N TOMMY'S MIND *he was swimming in the Atlantic Ocean and he was fifty miles from land.*
No one in their right mind wants to be in the custody of the local Police.

He was questioned by the Ranger (Officer Robert Johnson) on the way to their headquarters.
Tommy learned a lot answering the Ranger's questions and asking his own.
It appeared that the detective from Missouri (Officer Jenner), had mislead / lied about his purpose. The Ranger sounded as if he had felt manipulated.
Tommy talked continually during the trip to headquarters, he told the officer everything about his experience and how he had been released because he was not guilty of any crimes.

It seemed to Tommy that he was making headway with the Ranger but Officer Johnson was still a cop and he was not fully ready to trust Tommy's word over that of another officer of the law.
Officer Johnson also said a few things like, "you guys" and "People like you" which told Tommy that he may have entered medieval America.

Once in the Command Center Tommy was placed inside a detention room.
Tommy objected but as he was handed off from one officer to another, the worst communications became.
In Police custody everyone is guilty.

The room was abysmal. The walls had been scrawled on and were complete with dried liquid stains. The floors were linoleum and needed a mopping.

The only thing new in the room was the light bulb which illuminated all of its creepiness.

It was anytime from thirty minutes to an hour after being placed in the room when Officer Jenner was allowed to enter and question Tommy.

Seeing the man enter his small area, Tommy was, at first, worried.

Officer Jenner entered the room looking extremely stressed out and agitated.

"So, I told you that I would get your ass for something!! Now tell me where did you put the money"?

Tommy had been sitting on the wooden bench that also served as a cot. His bones were starting to ache just being cramped up in this room.

"Are you brain dead, replied Tommy, I DO NOT HAVE ANY MONEY!!!!!! AND I NEVER DID!!!!"

"Look Nigger, I will beat your monkey ass and then send you to real lockup where you will be used as a pin cushion everyday for the rest of your life....... where's the cash!!??"

Officer Jenner was bouncing from one foot to another intimating that he was ready to rumble. He stepped closer and closer to Tommy.

"This is the last time I am going to play this game with you. That dumb whore you were with did not have it. We have your buddies and the first one that talks gets a lighter sentence.

(he possessed the wide eye, large grin look of thief and liar. He looked around the room)

Listen, maybe you did just pick up that girl, and maybe you did not know about the bank heists.... but you saw the money and you took some... now didn't you"?

"Look Officer Jenner!!, you are dead wrong. You need to back up. I was never a part of their crime or knew anything about their crime or what, that woman, had in Her Bag"!!

"Stop lying Coon!!"
With this Officer Jenner moved closer and pushed Tommy into the wall.
With all his might and without thought, Tommy pushed back on Officer Jenner and he went flying across the short distance to the opposite wall, where he banged his head with a resounding thump.

Officer Jenner was now frantic and he charged over towards Tommy swinging and cussing.
At that very moment two Texas officers stepped into the small room and pulled Officer Jenner out.

"I want a lawyer!!!!! I want a lawyer NOW!!!!"
Tommy shouted with all the energy he could muster.

"Shut up nigger!!! we'll take care of you later."

When they closed the door Tommy's mind went into overdrive because he imagined he had just heard a threat which sounded like execution orders.
Tommy had read and known that in many areas of the United States a Caucasian could get a job on the police force with Klan membership. Somehow a Black or Hispanic would be unacceptable with gang membership in their folder but current Klan membership in a white officers folder is okay.
Why are there very few officers, if any, with Islamic names?
One thing that had been prevalent during this journey was that the newscast were full of Police complaint cases stressing Police brutality and murder. Everyday of Tommy's journey had been greeted by a new case from all over the country.
It was as if they (the police) were shooting Blacks for sport.
In all the cases there is hope that indictments will follow to reign in the kind of activity which has innocents, unarmed and handcuffed people dying everyday.
Once again Tommy was imagining him being one of those cases which go unreported and unknown for years to come.

His blood pressure was rising. He was trying to remain calm and not sweat or panic but he could not concentrate.

It took another hour or two.
When the Rangers opened the door to his cell Tommy tensed up.
He became real clear and focused.
One of the officers stepped in, "Come with me"!

Was this the okey-doke? When he stepped outside the cell were they going to beat him or kill him claiming he was running or being abusive.?

Tommy stepped cautiously and followed the officer down the hall where he was lead into another room.
This room was furnished with a comfortable sofa and several armchairs. There was a cocktail table with magazines and against the wall was a coffee maker with all the necessities on the table.

Tommy looked over the room.
There were two doors. The one he came through and another which lead to the officers working area.
There was a window which overlooked the area of the parking lot for visitor parking.
Tommy could see his car parked in the lot.

Officer Johnson walked into the room. Head held up marching to a beat in his skull.

"Mr. Williams I have discussed this with my commanding officer and in the spirit of Openness and Truth. There are no charges which we have found that warrant your arrest or further detainment. We would like to apologize for the inconvenience."

Tommy was silent for fifteen seconds before he blurted out, "That's my car outside!? Did you drive my car/ tow my car? Why? How do I know its not damaged?"

Officer Johnson sat with a partial grin but no words.

"I know that Officer Jenners is crazy. He made you violate my rights for no cause what-so-ever. I think he's on something because he's so jumpy. (Tommy looked directly into Officer Johnson's eyes)

I know he lied to you about me.

Where is that crazy Motherfucker? Is he going to pursue me down the road? Fuck this!! I want t file a complaint!!!!"

Tommy could see that his words were getting under Officer Johnson's skin. Common sense for Police is only seen when it is regimented. They walk a thin line.

It creates problems in their life. Alcoholism, Drug use, Divorce, Spousal and children abuse cases. It is a line only few can bear. It has been evident that most Police departments are not overloaded with exceptional people but of Human Beings will frailties, vices and desires.

It is said that one bad apple will spoil the barrel, that's what it likes when Police shield bad cops.

According to the law they all become accomplices in the murders, inefficiency, lies and corruption.

Officer Johnson had the look of someone opposed but compliant. He would do as told.

"Listen Mr. Williams, I do not know what you did to earn the mistrust of Officer Jenners but that is not my problem. Whatever situation you were exposed to its your problem, you should know that Officer Jenners did misrepresent you and overburden our department with actions unofficially performed.

(Officer Johnson returned Tommy's direct stare)

Personally, you may have a problem. You may be right, Officer Jenner does appear to be highly stimulated..... but he has been working tirelessly day and night trying to retrieve stolen money.

(Officer Johnson looked away again)

Officer Jenners may be personally involved in some illegal actions.

My department does not want the press or limelight of one of these cases. It is happening all over the country. Citizens are slandering and demeaning the Police establishment."

"Its easy to do, replied Tommy, when you are covering up for bad cops."

Officer Johnson's face turned beet red. He wanted to explode.
"You people ought to learn respect for the law"!!!!

"The law should be just and equal and then we all will be happy."

Officer Johnson stood up.

"Wait a minute!!! Its late (it was 10:30 pm). I could use a stay over at a local hotel. Plus, I have to be sure about my car.
I need to be guaranteed that it works, that it is not now loaded with illegal contraband.... I need to know where I am and how can I get out of here. SHIT!!! I'm Hungry!!!!"

Officer Johnson made bristling sounds. He was overloaded.
Tommy had to be careful not to go too far.

"If you will wait here I will get you your assurances and information. I will also return with your personal effects."
With that announcement Officer Johnson left the room.
A release of pressure engulfed Tommy's soul. He was over a hurdle. He was relieved.
He started thinking how or what he would do if confronted with Officer Jenners alone. He started making preparations in his mind. He moved his shoulders, arms and hands. He then raised his leg up, bent knee. He was testing his body.
This journey across the country now was officially two weeks long and he still was over fifteen hours away.
He was going to have to conserve energy. He took deep breaths and tried to center and calm his thoughts.
Why had he left the quiet, peaceful, ordinary tranquility of his West Philadelphia home? He tried to stop thinking.
Obviously they wanted him out of their center and their jurisdiction. It could jump off in the next ten minutes or it could take a few hours. He was all he had and he selfishly wanted to see tomorrow.

Relaxed and relieved Tommy drifted off into a quiet zone.
Tommy felt nuzzled soft and cozy in loving arms as he slept, outwardly he sat awkwardly on the couch balancing himself by holding on to the chair arm.

It was three thirty am when Tommy was waken by Officer Johnson.

"Mr. Williams, I have gotten you some coffee and a breakfast sandwich.
I have been assured by our mechanics that nothing is wrong with your car.
If there is a problem we can address it.
We did examine and search your car because we were lead to believe
that you were transporting illegal profits / contraband.
We found nothing in your car or amongst your belongings which
matched the descriptions we were searching for.
Your car has been restored to its original state."

Officer Johnson handed Tommy a bag with his personal belongings. A
cell phone started ringing.
Officer Johnson reached into his pocket and answered his phone.

Tommy stood up stretching his arms and legs. He placed the belongings
on the table while he picked up the coffee which had awaken him. It was
hot and instantly gave Tommy's system a jolt.
There were two egg and bacon sandwiches.
Tommy finished one just as Officer Johnson ended his phone call.

"Listen, said Officer Johnson. I have someone watching Officer Jenners
and I am going to accompany you, in another vehicle, to assure you and us
that Officer Jenners does not follow."

The cell phone rang again and Officer Johnson answered it.

Tommy was feeling pretty good.
The fact that they did anything concerning Officer Jenners was a
miracle. The second sandwich was even more satisfying. Tommy was starting
to relax. He felt wide awake and ready to start his journey.

Officer Johnson ended his second call and looked stunned at the table.

"You ate my sandwich too?"

"Sorry", replied Tommy with a good healthy grin.

Officer Johnson started spilling out.

"See this is my fault for getting involved with that Officer Jenners. I should have never listened to him. I should have thrown him into jail when I first came across him. Now, I have to clean this crap up. I have to escort you out of here, I had to arrange for someone to trail him and signal me, I had to stay up all day, last night and this morning.. I have to get the sarcasm from my lady because I was not there last night and now I have to starve because you have eaten my sandwich."

It was time to go.

17

O FFICER JOHNSON WAS *angry and boiling.*
On the way to the cars and throughout the inspection which Tommy gave his vehicle, Officer Johnson spoke.

He was upset with the newscasts from around the nation.
He was mad at the people for bringing light to what he considered a minor problem of corruption and racial politics.

Whenever Tommy countered with the numerous deaths of the unarmed and others in police custody he responded with, "Blunders... Bungles and botch's".
He seemed to think that in most of the cases the officer was in the right. He seemed to think that Police Officers were the cream of the crop.

Tommy wanted to talk about the numerous occasions where they, the police, witness injustice exercised by Politicians and big businessmen with impunity and their assistance.
Tommy could find no reason for the murders that were racking up this year and in many years gone by.
He had a lot to say to Officer Johnson but he knew he would be speaking to a deaf and dumb person.
The Ranger had already expressed his displeasure of his present duties and Tommy.
He seemed to be a good guy caught in a bad place. He was not going to admit the errors prevalent in the department that the department wouldn't acknowledge.

The car was fine. Tommy synched with his navigation system and it laid out the route to travel. Officer Johnson said he would follow.

Tommy was feeling good. He was brazen, the way he dealt with Officer Johnson.

He was seriously flirting with a fictional case based on the Ranger's temper as opposed to substantial charges.

Maybe Ranger Johnson was right, maybe 'we people' do have little respect for Law enforcement.

Hell, it was easy since they, the police, had less respect for our personal rights.

Tommy felt insulted and a little afraid because of that.

This year people are looking for indictments to establish some sanity with all the bad police work and mortal mistakes, it would as least show some semblance of reason and justice.

Now here he was with a dilemma; whenever he lost Ranger Johnson's company he was going to need a strategy on how to handle Officer Jenners if he reappeared.

Driving out west has proven to be quite an experience for Tommy.

The flat endless plains. Mountains off in the distance.

The sun is always up high and shining. The movement of the clouds and the twists of the road.

Tommy was fixated on white lines and broad landscapes.

Other thoughts kept Tommy tense.

What could he do?

Ranger Johnson was adamant that there would be no complaints filed or record made of this incident. Officer Jenners was informed by the department that Tommy would be released, he was also, according to Officer Johnson, verbally disciplined regarding his investigation.

Still, he was out there somewhere and if he showed up again threatening Tommy with violence, what was he going to do?

The thoughts made Tommy lose concentration of the road, once or twice. He was determined that he was not going to take a beating.

The sky was clear. There were few clouds and they drifted slowly but disappeared within minutes.

Ben E. King and the Drifters had been playing.

Tommy could hear the sounds. He remembered the words but his mind had been other places.

He noticed Officer Johnson a couple of times. He was driving a four door gray sedan.

He still had things he wanted to say to Officer Johnson.

Everyday more and more cases were being brought to light which show patterns of overzealous Police strategies. It would be one thing if a few cases existed but that was not reality.

In Tommy's mind the police, knowing his situation, should/could have done more to protect him from Jenners.

They were satisfied to turn their heads.

There was a space of purely Motown classics.

Stevie Wonder with "Fingertips", Smoky and the Miracles with "Choosy beggar", the Temptations with "I wish it would rain" and "Don't look back".

The Supremes started singing "Where did our love go" and finished with "Love Child".

Tommy felt energized.

The road traffic was light but brisk. At times a few trucks would move swiftly past Tommy in a caravan. In hindsight he would agree that the large Riggs ruled the highways.

Tommy was driving his Cadillac ATS. The majority of the vehicles were trucks carrying commerce, then there were pickup trucks of varying sizes and then there were Sport Utility Vehicles.

There were also classic vehicles peppered throughout his trip.

He noticed so much but couldn't concentrate on anything.

What was he going to do with a racist, drugged up, maniacal cop looking for him with a gun and a head full of erroneous assumptions?

He remembered that a few of the other officers had used racial epithets. This folks did not have the courtesy not to use racially offensive phrases to describe him.... how could they be depended on to safeguard him against another abusive white man?

Tommy lived his life not judging people by the color of their skin, their religion or favorite genre of music. He tried to judge everyone independently.

This at times was very problematic.

There are some people who just don't like you. These people are often beyond reason. Tommy is a person with a great deal of patience but there are folks who aggressively maintain ugly and abusive personalities which refuse to communicate, listen, compromise or reason.

Tommy found those folks to be extremely offensive and individually stunted intellectually.

Throughout his life Tommy has met many of these folks.

There is no shortage of assholes in life.

When Tommy categorized people he tried to do so by the content of their character.

One thing he was assured of...... it was that people will let you down.

There are so many levels upon which people can disconnect or never connect at all.

Tommy had a life full of ignorant people and situations. It is, he thought, impossible to live without experiencing the hypocrisy in the societies we live in.

It can even be hypothesized that living, coping and dealing with this knowledge is the core of living.

Human beings are vessels of conflicting emotions. The essence of these emotions cut across Joys and evils.

Physical joys of one can bring death to others. The sins of Ego can destroy the peace of others or it can create guidelines where everyone can experience freedom over their own lives.

Humans are so caught up in individual realities that they ignore the affects of their actions on others.

In this day and age, it can even be hypothesized that, people care less about each other and more on themselves.

This creates a world of selfish, ignorant, self righteous, stupid and often violent people.

In Tommy's opinion, being Black in America is a challenge by God to Stand up and represent truths.

Unacknowledged by many, the United States of America has benefited by the assimilation, creative and constructive efforts, ideas and belief in the falsehood that this is a free and fair country.

This country was not actually formed by the Europeans which came here and claimed everything. It was built and sustained by Indians that lived here before; by the slaves, their children and future heirs who being responsible for so much have received so little. This country was formed by the Immigrants who came here looking for a dream.

Tommy felt that he had to bow to no man. He tried to remain open.

He expected no one to be perfect. There were those who had accomplished more than him and he tried to accept their prowess without regret or excuse.

Throughout his life he had met people who were poor and caught in the system trying to define themselves through others. He had met the wealthy who enjoyed financial assets and advantages way beyond money. Each had a chance to create a better existence for themselves and others.

The dichotomy of the human soul is a battlefield.

Most people are fooled to assume that those of privilege and advantage must also be endowed with wisdom, intelligence charisma and righteousness.

In reality they are not always matched.

In an existence were so many lies have been constructed to validate rule by the guilty, greedy and ignorant.

In societies which claim that a college educated, social conscience, creative thinker can be second to a lazy, arrogant, violent person merely on the basis of skin color is the height of ridiculous fairy tales.... but it is the basis by which some folks live.

Money is the level that many people choose to communicate on.

As a young man, Tommy was used to being hated.

It appeared that many facets of the society was against him and for no better reason than hate politics which was designed to restrict citizens of color. It was a hateful continuance of the laws enacted to validate the sinful practice of Slavery.

Many of the people who hated him did not know him.

He was even hated by others in his community who did not love or respect themselves and who hated others who did not accept what they accepted as reality.

Tommy grew up in a house with a decent and rather extended sense of love and understanding. His parents were very religious but also very committed to being people of reason, intelligence and responsibilities.

Tommy learned early that there was more history to fill in the lessons taught in school. He learned that many of the haters were so because of their ignorance. It was a breakthrough of momentous proportions which did not eliminate the reality/ignorance which others still spread.

Tommy learned to stand up tall and be proud of his heritage because their struggle was one of truth and Spirit.

Tommy learned that to be able to believe in himself that he could not stand on his laurels. He needed to evaluate his life and his feelings daily.

His body was still sore. The cut would be around for a while, that scar was on his right arm.

He had some facial bruising that had disappeared.

There was some soreness in his ribs from hitting the ground during his tussle with Randy the bank thief.

The stop over in Oklahoma City had done a lot to heal his wounds.

He had been feeling pretty good before he had stopped at the bar.

Now after being in Police Custody again he could feel the stress draining what strength he had built.

The reality that he was being pursued by a violent idiot was bad enough but knowing that the police would not assist him was really frightening.

It was frightening because he knew he was going to have to act outside the box. It could lead to actions which may be construed differently. It was frightening because he had to contemplate his death in the equations. If he was going to die, he was going to defend himself and possibly kill.

He was starting to get tired.

It was amazing how when he was with Gene and partying with the women he had felt young and capable. Now that he was facing a rough encounter with actions that he may regret the rest of his life and he felt like the old person he was.

One thing for sure. He was not going to be bullying around by a rogue officer who had the wrong person in his sights.

No one was listening, not the Texas State Rangers and not Officer Jenners.

He could drive straight through, just stay awake, and drive the remaining fifteen hours.

No! to that, were his thoughts. He was already stressed.

GARRY JOHNSON

He could just see himself running off the road or worst causing an accident and deaths.

No! he was going to have to do this his way.... Do or Die.

Tommy never wanted to be white.

He had talked to a lot of people and read books and watched movies.

There were those that saw buying into a Caucasian American lifestyle was the epitome of getting over/ reaching it.

That never entered Tommy's brain.

It was never hard for Tommy to remember the harsh things White Americans have done to Black Americans. He was not in the habit of assigning blame for past transgressions onto people he did not know. He could not in earnest assign the blame of slave holders to his working buddies or just any white person he saw.

Now if they acted or said things which expressed an opinion which he found offensive he would speak on it.

If they disrespected him he returned the indignity with an emphasis on education, if possible, and self defense, if dealing with idiots.

He many times thought of what he discovered in a DNA search.

He had once, some years ago, taken a DNA test to investigate his heritage. He had some cousins but they were far removed and his father spoke rarely of other family, there were few Uncles and Aunts. The family even back then listed many who had passed on or who were unknown.

It was somewhat puzzling thought Tommy. He had never met his grandfather but he had a picture of a very dark, stern looking man with a lot of wild and wooly hair.

The only image he had of his grandmother was that of a matronly looking woman with those same hard penetrating eyes.

His father had told him that his grandfather was similar. They had come from North Carolina a few years after 1902.

They settled in North Philadelphia and Tommy's grandfather worked on the docks until his death after World War II.

Tommy's parents were examples of the older generation and they were industrious and intelligent enough to buy a home, raise a family and pass on the teachings of those before them.

That was when Tommy was first told of the true history of African Americans. He was not told hate. He was only taught history.

When he received his DNA results, it talked about the 18% Irish, 13% Portuguese and 9-10% Spanish ancestry on his paternal genes.

The only men in his family were Black man who provided a future for him complete with history and Pride.

The white genes which the tests discovered were, to him, another aberration of the white society which played sinful games onto his family. These genes belonged to people who had no place in his life. They were phantoms who tried to destroy those in his family.

For many years as a child he would hear the tales of missing black fathers. Tommy did not suffer from this but it was one of the lead-off accusations when haters talked about Blacks.

Tommy had seen all of the fun family, middle America family shows of his era. He thought he was Beaver but he was never white. The Cowboy movies, the spy, the science fiction, the action dramas/ books that became templates for his life never portrayed him as a white man.

The training/education Tommy received gave him hope, aspirations and righteousness as a Black man. The white genes he possessed came from deceivers.

No whites, except those DNA scientist, could detect his whiteness and to him it was not something he was proud of.

It represented, the worst part of him. He was not ashamed because of slavery or the brutal and savage lives that his black ancestors had to endure. He was proud of them... they were not at fault.

They were brutalized and still taught him love and wisdom.

Whites are blinded by the black skin and the lies to protect their advantages born from lies, violence, deception and ignorance.

They hate not for a reasonable point but basically because of their guilt.

They do not acknowledge our similarities, like the genes that link us all to Africa, they only see skin color.

Tommy never wanted to be white and he never regretted being who he was. Those European genes represented lies, hate, a lack of pride and esteem. He found these were his burdens to bear which he had to fight against. There was no pride in having those genes.

This whole thing with the Police, their brutality, the sentencing and judicial inequality reaches even beyond racial discrimination.

Tommy and the citizens of the United States were being used in a political game of control by forces more concerned with increasing their personal wealth.

The solutions were as plain as the open plains which Tommy was seeing through his car window.

The powers that be do not want the solutions.

They spend their time putting a spin on the truth so they don't confront the truth.

Those external forces are placing us all on a roller coaster of hate.

The same way the rich made their money, through fierce competition, lies, corporate spying, low salaries and subterfuge is what the rich have in store for the citizens when they control the government.

Sex, Race, Gender and even age are used to create conflict in the politics of control. Issues are coded in lies. Solutions are based on who has the advantage not efficiency or morality.

Tommy's head was spinning.

What was he going to do. He had never owned a gun or wanted one. There were places were he could buy a weapon. He had seen more than a few in his travels.

He thought maybe he should have gone to the shooting complex back in Oklahoma.

Yet if he had a gun he was going to have to use it.

Shooting a Police officer would certainly have him vilified.

The reality was that no one really cared.

He was the victim of illegal and unauthorized abuse. His attacker carried a gun and was totally psychotic. He was innocent.... and no one cared.

Maybe he should at least try again to solicit some legal criminal enforcement and judicial assistance in the next town.

If he could find some legal assistance he would not have to worry about doing something that might be misconstrued.

In his life, asking the Police for help was dangerous. It was not that they were always wrong it was more that they were less than diplomats and more agents of complication.

Officer Johnson made a point of establishing eye contact.

Up ahead was the Texan border, this was the end of his journey.

He expressed a stern passing glance and then veered off finding his exit to return home.

The oldies were still pumping music into the vehicle.

James Brown, The main Ingredients, The Dells and the Delfonics had just ended. Barbara Acklin, Mary Wells and Barbara Mason followed them.

The ikettes were playing when he made up his mind and was prepared to take his next step.

He was going to explore his options, buy the things he needed and get a good night's sleep.

The sun looked a little different and the passing of time seemed extremely poignant.

He was in trouble. He was on his own.

In the hood, the hype is that everyone is tough. The truth is that very few were tough but it is the mindset of urban existence.

Today, right now, Tommy felt tough.

He was going to represent himself in his image of himself.

He was prepared to stand up against the Insanity and he was prepared for the worst.

GARRY JOHNSON

9+9

TUCUMCARI, NEW MEXICO was the first fair sized city which Tommy passed through after crossing the border with Texas. The city was founded in 1901.

This was the site of a railroad camp which was originally called Ragtown and Six Shooter Siding.

The name was changed in 1908 and it is the same as the mountain which is nearby.

Tommy wanted to make some phone calls and buy some things to carry out his plan, if Officer Jenners showed up.

He had reached the city yesterday afternoon.

After a restful night's sleep he went out into the town to purchase the items he needed.

Tucumcari is an attraction on route 66. It is a small town known for its history and many motels. Tommy decided to stay at one of the newer chain motels rather than the older vintage ones he had passed.

He was not interested in the history or sightseeing. He was still somewhat nervous and very cautiously watching his surroundings.

He wanted to see Officer Jenners coming.

The city of Tucumcari is just that though. It is little more than an attraction.

There are numerous motels and a few hotels. Everything is basically directed towards tourist and trucker traffic.

One thing which Tommy wanted to buy was a camcorder.

He estimated that he needed such a camera to possibly record any actions and maybe even confessions by Officer Jenners.

All of the reports Tommy was reading about Police brutality and the protests which were being held to draw attention gave Tommy the idea.

There were groups pushing for the Police to carry video devices and citizens were being urged to record any actions which they felt were suspect. It was being touted as a method to safeguard justice and support the words of witnesses and the Police.

Tommy had decided against buying a gun.

If Jenners did show and if things did get heavy, owning a gun was not going to go in Tommy's favor.

He planned to confront Jenners in a conversation which he was going to set the camcorder to record.

He planned on trying to draw Jenners attention to him because he was going to be holding up his cell phone, claiming to be recording Jenners actions.

He figured that if or when Jenners tried to stop him from recording that he would not notice the additional device.

He finally found an affordable miniature action based camcorder that skateboarders use to record their actions. The camera also offered a remote to start and stop the camera.

That was earlier today.

After reading the instructions manual, Tommy had taken some pictures outside of Tucumcari Mountain.

He thought about going to the dinosaur museum.

He was starting to relax a little.

Amazingly enough, Tommy had a restful sleep.

He was not burdened by dreams/ nightmares.

His body was healing and he felt that the wide open spaces and clean air was benefiting his recovery.

It was going to take him another thirteen to fifteen hours to reach Los Angeles, another hour and a half to the house in Thousand Oaks.

He needed to have the least amount of stress on his mind when he arrived to talk with his daughter and wife.

GARRY JOHNSON

Another facet of Tommy's plan involved Gene.

He had called Gene yesterday.

Tommy caught Gene on his way to a familiar hang out.

Gene said he was going there to meet a new woman he had met.

It was always the same with Gene.

What Tommy requested of Gene was complicated. Everything with Gene always was.

Tommy had remembered what Gene had told him about his Uncle's association with a right wing group of law enforcement and political representatives back there in the St. Louis area.

What Tommy suggested was that Gene call his Uncle and find out if he could get someone to recall Jenners from his personal quest to make Tommy's life hell.

The two men talked quite a while.

Gene offered to join Tommy. Tommy refused his companionship. He still had other issues to deal with.

Gene was angry and quite belligerent. He talked about all the cases surfacing across the country and how he hated the arrogant bullshit that the law enforcement agencies were saying.

He spouted off for nearly forty minutes until Tommy could reign him in and he repeated his request.

Gene agreed to call his Uncle. He was not sure just how far his uncle's influence reached but he was willing to do anything to help.

He then started again trying to convince Tommy to meet him at the Albuquerque airport.

Tommy thanked Gene for offering and for his help but emphasized that he had made some other plans in case Officer Jenners showed up.

It was a long shot but Tommy was willing to try anything that could/ would alleviate a confrontation.

That was yesterday and Tommy was hoping that it help.

Regardless, Tommy still cautious.

Tommy had stepped outside his room to purchase a sandwich from a nearby shop he had seen.

He was going back to his room, eat his sandwich, drink some bourbon and beer. He was contemplating his journey.

He had Albuquerque, Flagstaff and finally Los Angeles left.

The sound of a motorcycle broke his concentration and as he turned to see from where, he was greeted by the phrase "Fuck the Motherfucking Police"!!"

It was Biggs from the bar.

"So I see you beat their bogus rap..... I knew you were a smooth operator", shouted Biggs.

"Damn", replied Tommy, as he walked over to Biggs.
"I wanted to thank you for picking up my bill at the bar."
Tommy reached into his pocket for his wallet to repay Biggs for his favor.

"Screw that Brother..... what's that you've got there"?

Tommy looked at the sandwich and six pack of beer in his grasp.

"I was just going to go inside, eat this sandwich and have a few drinks.... why don't you join me"?

"Hell yeah"!! replied Biggs as he maneuvered to park his bike.

Inside the room Tommy laid out the sandwich on the dining table and the room. He placed the beers on the table and went into the bathroom where he retrieved two plastic cups and the liter bottle of Kentucky whiskey he had chilling on ice.

Biggs sat down in the chair with the heavy force of a big man and preceded to open a bottle of beer and guzzle it down.
Biggs reached into his shirt pocket and brought out a rolled joint.
"You mind"? He asked
"Not at all" replied Tommy.

Biggs removed the light leather jacket he was wearing and tossed it onto the bed.
He settled in and drank down the liquor that Tommy had poured out into a cup for him.
He drank the booze and emitted a sound much like clearing one's throat.

Tommy split the sandwich and the two men ate, drank and relaxed.

Tommy and Biggs talked while they shared the marijuana joint that Biggs had provided.

Biggs was in the area because he had picked up a trucking gig.
He had to go to a nearby depot and take over for a driver who had taken ill. He explained that he was on his way when he thought he saw Tommy's car and he decided to investigate.

Tommy was not sure if it was the liquor or the joint but Biggs started talking about his life.
He explained that his mother had married a dark complexion Hispanic years ago.
He said he liked the guy and that he had a little brother because of their bond.
He said that he noticed some kids giving him a hard time because of his complexion and how he hated bullies.
As he talked about his temper and how it had gotten him into trouble with the cops. He said, "If those motherfuckers ever treated my brother the way I see them treat others I would whup their asses."
It was a little frightening but Biggs was if anything straight forward so Tommy relaxed and got wasted.
Tommy told Biggs about his journey, how he was going to reunite with his wife at his daughters house in California.
He made it sound like more of an ultimatum he was going to deliver because he wanted to spread his wings and live a little.

Biggs talked about his relations with women... mostly no good hoochies and prostitutes was how he described them.
He was attached to his mother but he also described her as a handful of rattlesnakes.
That was part of the reason he liked her husband because he was someone who was able to control her crazy.
Marriage was not for him, he was sure.

The bottle was more than half empty when Biggs pulled another marijuana joint from his pocket.

At this point Tommy was assured that he was not leaving today.
He opened the two remaining beers when there was a knock at the door.

Tommy cautioned Biggs to cover the joint.
"I was just going to call the desk and tell them I won't be checking out until tomorrow", he said as he walked towards the door.

As Tommy was opening the door, it was being shoved towards him and he backed up trying to stand.... but he fell.

In stepped Officer Jenners slamming the door closed, Gun drawn pointed squarely at Tommy lying on the ground.
"I told you I would get you scumbag"!!

"You better put that piece away" bellowed Biggs.

Officer Jenners had not noticed the man seated at the table but once he did he was hard to ignore because Biggs had out his 45 caliber handgun and pointed it squarely at Officer Jenners.
"So your his contact"?, said Jenners.

Tommy crawled backwards on the floor and pulled himself up on the bed.
He was able to start the camcorder running which had been sitting on the table next to the bed.
Tommy also pulled his telephone out of his pocket and aimed it towards Jenners.

"Put that shit away, said Jenners, give me what I want and I will let the two of you go."!!

"Listen you sick shit. If you do not lower that gun from me and my buddy I am going to blow your fucking head off."

The threat from Biggs forced Jenners to reconsider who to aim at.

GARRY JOHNSON

"I know you bastards have the loot. Its mine. Your pal Randy is not the real brain. Now hand it over and live or I'll shoot you both and have you both arrested and locked away forever."

"You dumb cop, shouted Tommy, I told you before that I don't have your money. I just gave that woman a ride. I was never a part of any plot to steal money or rob a bank. I dare you to call the cops. You have no jurisdiction here. Leave me alone"!!!

"Do what my friend says or I will blow your ass away" echoed Biggs.

The air was becoming super heated in the room.
It might have been the booze.

Tommy's hand was shaking and that's when he noticed that he had not started the recorder in the telephone.
He turned it on.

Jenners still had his gun pointed at Tommy but he was starting to sweat because Biggs frightened him.
The moment he swung the gun around to aim it at Biggs he feared he would be shot.

A telephone started ringing.

Everyone froze in silence.

"Answer your phone, said Biggs, It might be the last chance you have to repent before you die."!

Jenners clumsily took his phone from his jacket pocket.

"Speak, he said, Captain!, yes sir... but but Captain........ I... I... Captain I can explain..... No Sir.... No Sir...... I ..... I.... but Captain I can..............".

It must have been some conversation because Jenners was visibly shaken and his concentration was waning.

Jenners never completed a sentence.

"No Sir, I haven't.......... Yes Sir........... Yes Sir......... but Captain I............ Yes Sir I am returning now."

Jenners placed the phone carefully back into his pocket.
His eyes were full of confusion and he had lowered his gun and was placing it back into its holder.

He looked directly towards Tommy.
"I don't know how you did it or who you know but one day you will cross my path again and my hands won't be tied then."

"But right now, said Biggs, you are going to take your sad ass out of here and don't come back again.... because, if I see you I will shoot."

Biggs was still holding his gun pointed directly at the frustrated officer.
Jenners sneered at Biggs, "I don't know who you are but you will get yours."

With those last words Jenners reached back and twisted the doorknob, leaving the room by slamming the door.

Tommy was still holding his phone and Biggs still had his gun out but there were no words.
After a few seconds of silence, Biggs said, "Damn Man, I'm thirsty, let's finish this bottle and get some more."!

Tommy looked at the camcorder and it was still recording.
He walked over to the table and lit the joint that Biggs had taken out.
Biggs was downing a good two ounces of whiskey.

"That was deep" said Tommy.

"I was going to laugh when you called him a 'Dumb Cop'" said Biggs.

The two men laughed. Was it nervous tension, the making of a friendship or just the fact that they both were wasted?, it didn't matter.

GARRY JOHNSON

20

AFTER FINISHING THE bottle and the joint, Tommy and Biggs were preparing to go out and purchase some more liquor when again a telephone rang.

This time it was Biggs.

"Yeah, said Biggs, Sure I want the job!!, I'm on my way now.!! keep your pants on"!!

That ended what was assuredly going to be a monster session of drunkenness.

Biggs and Tommy exchanged phone numbers.
The run Biggs had accepted would take him to San Francisco.
Tommy knew he was too drunk to drive and he could only imagine that the journey was going to be challenging for Biggs.
Regardless, Biggs stood up without a wobble, he placed his jacket on. He looked at his image in the wall mirror and ran his fingers through his hair. His eyes were not red but they were distant looking.
Biggs told Tommy to come back after he finishes with his wife.
Tommy was seriously considering it.
A future with Eloise was doomed. It did not matter what he wanted, he was never going to be able to work things out with her.

Everything being said Biggs walked out.
The sound of his motorcycle boots hitting the floor seemed louder.
Tommy was starving.

He went to the front desk and paid for another night. There were fliers for businesses which delivered food to the motel.

Tommy grabbed a fistful and slowly walked back to his room.

Had Officer Jenners chose to surprise Tommy it would have been all over, but it was all over. Officer Jenners was gone for good.

Tommy ordered some fried chicken and fries once he returned to his room.

He finally stopped the camcorder from running.

It had caught Jenners image and him holding his weapon. The angle of the shot caught him and the space behind him, it did not record Biggs image or Tommy, except for his leg/ arm which crossed the lens a few times.

He fell asleep in what could only be considered a drunken state of bliss. There was no pain and only endless hours of comfortable, satisfying, tranquil sleep.

There was sunshine and love in his dreams and he wanted to stay there hugging the warm flesh of the beautiful woman clinging to him, making him happy.

Unknown to him there was joy in Charlotte, North Carolina and he was being thought of in a fond manner.

Everyone had thought Tommy had skimmed money from the bank heist where in reality, Denise had.

Before returning to Tommy's room she had made a package of bills, wrapped it up and mailed it to her postbox in Charlotte.

Denise had been honestly sorry to have involved Tommy in her scheme but in her mind she had to do what she could for her and her daughter.

Denise thought of Tommy. He was different. He cared about people. He was kind. She had not made love to any man in years the way she allowed herself to love him. He deserved more and personally she could use it herself.

They would never meet again but she would never forget the man who helped her get what was owed her from Jazmine's father.

Tommy awoke surrounded by food on the bed.

He was happy and energized. This he thought would be the last stop he would make before reaching California and his family.

As he started his journey, the music from the soundtrack of "Shaft" was playing. Tommy smiled, he felt like a "Bad Mother... Watch your mouth... just talking about Shaft.... and you can dig it."

The sun was beaming bright and it felt warm.

There was something in the air and the tranquil beauty of the land that filled Tommy.

So much had happened since he started this trip. He could relive the routes he took and remember the hours spent with Gene.

They had together seen some startling landscapes but Tommy had been blow away with everything he had seen since Oklahoma.

New Mexico and Arizona were states where it only became more of a peaceful journey.

The Carlsbad caverns are probably the best known tourist site in New Mexico. The state is basically viewed as a desert but there are also eighty-eight mountain ranges.

The Manzano, Ladron and South Baldy ranges reach three thousand feet about sea level and the Sandia Crest reaches four thousand feet.

The Rocky Mountains and several rivers cross the state and make them special points of viewing when in the state.

Tommy read about the terrain on his travel maps. Even though he used the navigation information from the service attached to his car, Tommy still carried the travel and road map he picked up at the gas station. He felt more confident following the directions in the car when he had some idea where he was going.

He saw branches of the Canadian and Pecos rivers and he believed he saw the Rio Grande.

Tommy's mind and concentration went from landscape to the music playing to what he was going to tell Eloise.

He found it difficult not wondering what activities Gene or Buggs were engaged in.

More than once he thought about Denise's body.

There were reminders in the landscape and the music.

Arizona has two hundred and ten mountain ranges and several national forests, Parks and monuments.

The Grand Canyon and large Ponderosa Pine Forest are also attractions in Arizona.

Tommy passed by the Kaibab and Tonto national Forest.

He remembered reading that, during WW2, there was a German POW camp and a Japanese-American Interment camp in the state.

There had been so much history in these lands out west.

Tommy again thought of the Buffalo Soldiers.

In 1870 they had a base camp in the Guadalupe Mountains which Tommy believes he passed when he left Texas and entered into New Mexico.

He remembered that their last home was Camp Lockett and that they also had been housed in the Wichita Mountains (fort Sill) and Fort Davis (Texas).

They were the 9th and 10th Cavalry Regiments or the 24th and 25th Infantry Units. They chased Geronimo in Arizona and the Cheyenne in Kansas. They were also active in the Apache wars of the late 1870's and early 1880's.

They represented another facet of living in a racist country.

They were the first African American soldiers allowed in the regular Army, post slavery.

They staked their claim on citizenship by serving their country.

Similar to the treaties and negotiations that the country had made with the native American Indians; the acceptance of the African American was not legally given until the passage of the Civil Rights bill in 1964 and 1968 and the voting rights act of 1965.

The service of the Buffalo Soldier caused humiliation for the soldiers within their own communities and even their relationship with the American Indian.

There was limited occupational mobility and their service often put them at personal risk.

There are several well known cases of African American Soldiers being beat, abused or killed by whites who resented their service /wearing of the uniform.

The Military has even hung, executed or discharged soldiers who defended themselves or others from such attacks.

The history of those men are written all over the western territories where they worked preventing the 'Boomers' from entering or trying to settle in the Indian territories.

These thoughts filled his head as he passed miles and miles of open territory.

He still did not know what exactly he was going to say to Eloise.

This trip started with that in mind and now almost seven and a half hours away from seeing her and he was clueless.

He and she had lost so much. How could he even tell her about the full adventure of the journey? It was going to be impossible talking about the sore points in their relationship.

He knew that any real personal information he would divulge would be questioned and criticized.

Why did he spend so much time in Oklahoma city? How did you meet Biggs? What exactly did he and Gene do? How long did they stay there? And why would he drive across the country alone?

How was he going to explain his healing knife wound?

Even if he was healing he was still aching from time to time, depending how he sat or how he leaned.

Resting his arm on the armrest in the car reminded him of hitting the floor when Jenners barged into his room.

He had been speculating in his mind that Tiffany was just being his daughter. She may have no real reason to want to see her father than that. Its possible that her mother was being annoying, Mothers and Daughters have strange relationships.

It was most likely, he thought, that Tiffany just wanted to get her parents together.

She may be involved with a white guy but she knew that information wouldn't phase him.

Tommy and Eloise never preached racial hate and the women were not interested in Politics.

Whomever Tiffany chose was going to meet her standards or they were in trouble.

Tiffany was very industrious and independent. No matter what she had said about being out of work for a year, Tommy knew she would be working within weeks.

It was a reality about women that Tommy seemed to notice.

Tommy had many friends from work with children and he had noticed many of the families in his neighborhood.

It appeared to him that more of the women were focused on earning great wealth than the men.

Sure men want great wealth but most men will find that peaceful place where they earn enough to do what they want.

Women never have enough.... they can always spend more money.

The world has changed and women are capable of earning great wealth without the need of a man. Most women who earn good money and have great independence will work tirelessly to earn more. Women have always been prime workers throughout history and being able to be ably compensated is an aphrodisiac more seductive than great love or hot sex.

Tiffany had a challenging job and she always was looking for new horizons.

"Wow!!, thought Tommy, maybe she is contemplating moving to another city or taking a job outside the country."

The sun was moving across the sky.

Tommy was mesmerized by its scenic beauty. As it became darker and the sun finally set, Tommy once again found himself deep in thought.

Today Tommy had gone through Albuquerque, Gallup, Flagstaff, Kingsman, the Mojave National Preserve, San Bernardino and now, Los Angeles.

He had started his journey between ten and eleven a.m. and it was now 2:00am of the following day.

This trip would take him along the Ventura Freeway pass Sherman Oaks, Calabassas and finally to Thousand Oaks.

Tommy contemplated stopping in L.A. and getting a room for overnight.

He remembered that the house was also close to Simi Valley and whether the reports were true or not he did not want to be stopped by any overzealous police officers patrolling the area.

The house was not located in a gated community. It was still a very quiet one where sensor lights spring to life during any movement.

Tommy pulled up into the driveway and parked his car outside of the two car garage. He thought of calling and alerting his family that he was outside.

The door key was on the key ring with his car key.

It was 3:45am, he tried his key into the lock. The door opened effortlessly. He stepped in.

The home alarm wasn't on.

He walked into the very spacious downstairs family area and sat down on the sofa.

He stared around the room. It was as he remembered it with maybe a new addition here or there.

Sitting there he realized that he should have done something to alert Eloise and Tiffany. He did not want to startle them.

He was seated in an area where he was visible once they came down the stairs. He settled back into the soft cushioned sofa, it had been a long drive and he had struggled to stay awake.

When he opened his eyes, Eloise was standing before him with her arms crossed, wearing a scowl and complaining.

"So you finally showed up", said Eloise with a distasteful smirk on her face.

Tommy sat up. He had a blanket over him.

"That's right, continued Eloise, your daughter came down here and put that blanket on you. You were down here snoring like some bear. You were lucky that we did not shoot your dumb ass!

Why didn't you phone us and let us know you would be here?"

Tommy straightened up. He could feel some soreness in his arm and his side was a little tender.

He must have made a distinctive face because Eloise said, "Now what's wrong with you"?

"I was just sleeping on an angle", responded Tommy.

"I was trying not to wake you two, I got in at close to four this morning."

It was at that point that Tiffany entered from the next room.
She was dressed for her morning walk /run.
She walked over and sat next to her father, placing a kiss on his cheek.

"Is this how you two say hello? (Tiffany looked at both her parents) Its a good thing you remembered how to unarm the alarm."

"The alarm was off" responded Tommy.

"Mom"!? Tiffany once again looked towards her mother.

"I told you I can't work that thing, said Eloise, I can never set the alarm."

"But Mom... what if I am out over night."?

"Nobody is coming in here and if they do I know how to call the police and scream."

"But Mom"

"And if all else fails, continued Eloise, I know where you hide that gun you have."

Tommy looked at his daughter.

Tiffany stood up and walked over to stand next to her mother.

"Dad, why don't you get your clothes out of the car, take a shower, get something to eat. You and Mom can talk all day. Tonight, we'll have a big dinner here together so I can tell you both something I need to say."

Tommy and Eloise looked at each other.
He could see a blank look his wife's eyes. She was as clueless as he was.

After unloading his bags into the third bedroom, Tommy showered, shaved and slept the sleep of a peaceful king.
The kingdom was at peace and there were no wars on the arising.
He had endured some harrowing developments during his trip.

GARRY JOHNSON

The journey which was to have only lasted a week had extended into four. He had not packed for such a long journey and he was in need of freshly laundered clothes.

He had planned on a short nap and then a trip to a local store to purchase a new outfit.

That never materialized.

Once Tommy woke up, he noticed that it was six thirty.

Dinner had been scheduled for around seven or seven thirty.

In the closet were a pair of clean jeans and a shirt Tommy had left from a previous visit.

He and Eloise had chosen separate rooms back then.

When Tommy came downstairs he noticed some people leaving.

He came to discover that they were the caterers. Tiffany had the dining room majestically set, everything was exquisite.

He felt somewhat out of place in his blue jeans and short sleeved safari shirt.

Eloise was attired in a magnificent looking pants suit. She and Tiffany had been clothes shopping and this was her first opportunity to wear it.

The three sat around making small talk. Tommy was drinking his favorite bourbon in a finely cut crystal glass.

In about twenty minutes the door bell rang.

Tiffany, who was also adorned in a very soft pastel pants suit with a blouse that large sleeves answered the door. When she walked it made her appear to be a butterfly.

Chadwick Winslow is a man of about thirty eight years of age. He stands about six feet and weighs close to one hundred and eighty pounds. He greeted us all with a big beaming smile.

He also presented Tiffany and Eloise with flowers and kisses.

He was dressed in beige slacks, a white shirt and a blue suit jacket.

Introductions were made by Tiffany and after a moment of small chatter the four people went into the dining room to enjoy dinner.

The meal was extremely well done.

Everything was superb. The wine which was a part of the meal was in itself, a wonder to behold.

Chadwick, or Chad as he preferred, and Tiffany had met during one of Tiffany's business assignments.

In fact, Chad, owned a business which catered to the rich California homeowner and their needs for construction/Security.

Eloise was all smiles and charm. Tommy felt like he had entered another dimension of milk and honey. He was taken by Eloise's beauty and the calm demeanor of her presence.

The time had come and Tiffany stood up.

"Mom and Dad, I wanted you both here because I have an announcement and because you are the people I love, I feel obligated to include you both."

Tiffany held out her hand and Chad rose and stood beside her.

"Chad and I are very much in love. He has asked me to marry him and I have accepted. (a tear rolled down Eloise's face)

We have talked about raising a family and we are both so happy together.

We have decided, to before we get married, take a trip abroad for several weeks. We need to experiment what it takes to live together and to travel a little before we have children.

We have witnessed that marriage is a commitment that withers in many. We want desperately to make the right decisions.

Mom and Dad, I know that you have had your own personal problems. I love you both and without you I am lost. I pray that you can work out those problems.

I would like you both to live here for the four to five months that Chad and I are abroad. I hope the California sunshine and wine can bring you closer together because I will need you both to help raise your grandchildren."

Eloise and Tommy looked at each other.

"My parents, said Chad, are divorced and very much enemies in separate camps. Tiffany has expressed nothing but love and respect for you. In many ways she has said that she hopes we can remain together as long as you have."

GARRY JOHNSON

Eloise said, "How proud she was of Tiffany and that she wished them nothing but good fortune and happiness in their life together."

A telephone started ringing.
Tommy was echoing Eloise's sentiments.
The telephone continued to ring.

Chad excused himself and took out his cell phone.
The telephone kept ringing.

Eloise shouted, "Tommy is that you"?

Startled, Tommy reached into his pocket and pulled out his phone.
The caller I.D said it was Gene.

He had not talked to him since he called asking for his uncle's help.

"Excuse me, said Tommy, one moment."

"Hey man, Look I meant to call you and thank you for calling your uncle. It worked, but right now I am going to have to call you back."
There was a lot of static or mumbling.
No, Tommy could sense something else.

"Excuse me", said Tommy and he arose from the table and walked into the next room.

"Yo, Man... what's happening?! Are you crying. Did something happen"?

Eloise called from the dining room, "Tommy whoever it is tell them you will call them back."!!

"One minute"!!!, he replied

"Gene what's up"?

"She dead man, she was only twelve years old. She was a good girl. She never hurt anyone how can she be penalized for where she lives."!!!!

"Gene, what are you talking about? Who is dead? What happen"?

Tommy turned his head and could see Eloise standing at the entrance way to the dining room giving him the stink eye.

He put up one finger.
She made a face at him which said, "Fuck You"!! and then she put a big grin on her face and turned around and re-entered the dining room.

"Her mother took her to her grandmother's house in Cleveland.
She was playing with her friends when the Police mistook the address for another. They barged in, breaking everything in sight.
She was just frightened. She screamed and they shot her.
She's dead man... She's dead......... Listen man, I need you.
You are the only one I can depend on. I can't do this by myself.
They are going to pay for this...... I'm going to kill that Motherfucker"!!!

"Listen Gene, I'm really speechless, my condolences. Listen this won't stand. They will prosecute him...."

"Tommy, I need you man. I am not waiting for some grand jury to exonerate this fool. How often does that happen!!! I'm going to get my own justice. She was my daughter!!! What if it was your daughter?...... I need your help man... I will do the deed but I need your help....."

"Gene don't do anything. I'll be there. Wait for me in Philly".

"Tommy call me when you get to Cleveland.... I'll be there."

The phone call ended and Tommy was nervous and shaky.

He turned around again and this time he saw Chad standing near the entrance way.

"I am sorry, said Tommy. I am so happy for you and Tiffany. I don't want to take anything away from this moment for you two.... in fact, it is a happy moment for us all and I welcome you to the family."

The two men re-entered the dining room where Eloise and Tiffany sat chatting.

Tommy raised his glass of expensive, delicious wine and toasted to the happiness and prosperity of their family.

They continued their discussion of the trip Tiffany and Chad were planning. The night was filled with joy and bubbles.

In the back of Tommy's mind was the grief and misery that Gene was going through.

He was lucky, his daughter was going to marry a very nice man and she was planning on starting a family.

A family of inter-racial children in a world of racial ignorance and hatred. He wanted more than ever to be around for them, to help them overcome the lunacy around them.

It was not an option for Gene's daughter. She was dead and he was planning on something that Tommy could only see as suicide.

Gene had been there for him. What could have happened had not he called his uncle?

Who was he if he did not stand beside his friend? A friend who had stood beside him.

He was not a politician or a soldier but wasn't justice due for the dead body of this dead twelve year old girl and her parents?

He was not sure what he could do. He could keep Gene out of trouble and alive or they both could wind up dead/imprisoned.

Now that there was the promise of his own grandchildren Tommy wanted very much to remain alive and free.

One thing was obvious, Tommy was not thinking about confronting Eloise with his own speech of freedom.

He and she had lived together and apart for so long that he could endure whatever was left, especially if it made his family happy, healthy and stronger.

He and Eloise talked about sharing the home in California during Tiffany and Chad's trip around the world. Living together yet apart was not going to be a problem. Maybe they might reach some suitable compromise.

Tommy knew how to handle this. All he had to do first was survive whatever happened once he met up with Gene.

If he was going to be anything to himself, for his family and his grandchildren, he was going to stand up as a man for what he thought was right.

In the name of Justice for all that his life would ever mean to anyone Tommy swallowed his personal desires and chose to challenge the wind.

Tiffany and Chad had not made any specific plans because they had been waiting for the opportunity to get everyone on-board.

Tommy explained that he needed to take care of a few things at the house in Philadelphia.

He had only planned to leave for a short time and he now needed to secure the house for a longer stretch.

Chad had explained to him that he could take from a couple of weeks to a month. He still had arrangements that he also had to secure for his own home and his business.

Tommy decided to leave his car behind in California. No one wanted him to drive across country again.

Chad gave Tommy a credit card to cover any plane trips, hotel arrangements or car rentals that he required.

He had overheard some of Tommy's responses to the telephone conversation in which Cleveland was mentioned.

Chad did not know what Tommy had to do. It could have been a mistress, he did not care. He wanted desperately to impress his future father in law. He explained that it was a business card he would authorize for any of his sales staff. He encouraged Tommy to spend without conscience or limit.

As Tommy boarded the plane his mind was filled with all the possibilities of a life of happiness with grandchildren, of Tiffany's joyful promise, life near the California beaches under the west coast sun. He thought of a world where he could live without prejudice, poverty or hate.

He would first go to Philadelphia and take care of his affairs then he would be off to be the man he told himself he was. He was going to make a stand for Justice.. whatever it took.

*I*N THE NAME *of Justice.*
WWII was fought against a foe who trampled human rights, vilified a whole race of people as the evil of the world and exterminated innocent victims.

Today unarmed men, women and even sleeping children are murdered and their assailants are exonerated and free to continue to harass, intimidate and even kill those in police custody without sanction.

Today Representatives of the people manipulate the laws while ignoring and removing the ability of citizens to represent and govern themselves.

Propaganda is being spread. Out right Lies.

It represents a race of citizens as the evil demons among mankind, when in reality they represent the killing of sheep and not the gun toting, military style aggressors which roam the streets judging the innocent by color.

In the name of Justice

There is one thing that the European Slave trade did create which will live on in Prosperity and Greatness

Its prime purpose was to create a wage-less society of servants to pick the gum off the sidewalks and marvel at the ingenuity of their benefactors.

It was created to satisfy a lust for power and demigods.

It was done to organize and explain the universe in one voice by one voice.

Slavery provided sex for troubled and decadent men.

It gave disposable workers to bend, break and kill on all of the Industrial, Architectural and other dangerous ventures which occur in the making of a nation from a colony and creating an Empire.

Slavery was meant by some to honor God by erecting the Earth towards the heavens.

Manifest Destiny was meant to legitimize theft and deception.

Throughout it all Slaves ran away and Revolted.

Even after the robber barons were no longer allowed to offset the system by using unpaid slave labor; once they could no longer insure the lives of slaves as property to recoup their treachery; when it was no longer possible to create an empire built and operated by slaves for slave owners, there were those that wanted to destroy the former slaves through social leprosy.

The former slave proved to be resilient; after seeing them rise to levels of lawyers and doctors, after seeing that they were formidable competitors for the jobs which drive a nation; they were set upon with lies.

Oppressors created laws and lawless disorder to restrict man, women and children of color from participating in American life.

They were removed from the textbooks, incarcerated for unemployment, poverty and vagrancy.

They were belittled in all forms of media and ignored and denied even justice for the loss of their lives when whites wanted the air they breathed.

The foul taste of those times still smell today more than two hundred years after the abolition of the slave trade and the emancipation of all slaves in the United States.

There is still a massive problem in this country dealing fairly with all citizens.

There are racial divides and differences in the servicing of freedom in this country.

Some talk about the immigration problem when actually the problem is how we treat people born and raised here.

In the name of Justice

The situation was and always existed that people cannot be slaves.

Slaves are people who will one day seek appreciation and recognition of their lives. It has recurred time and time again in history.

GARRY JOHNSON

The European Slave Trade meant to create a new person. It sought to devalue a race of people. It tried through force and fear to duplicate God's might and wisdom. It Failed.

It was always Immoral and unethical and it proves hundreds of years since it ceased to still present problems.

The Slave Trade, slavery and the creation of the KKK and Jim Crow Laws was meant to destroy the African American race.

What has come out of it is all within the history of African Americans. Anyone who gets a comprehensive and knowledgeable retelling of history will see the greatness and inspiration that the history of African Americans show.

The Accomplishments, Achievements and Contributions of African American continually enhance and increase the legend.

Through an attitude forged in barbaric times and modified throughout contemporary times a new America will be created and the history of the Slaves will be the template of strength, resilience and genius which will move the United States and the world into a better tomorrow.

All In the name of Justice.

www.ingramcontent.com/pod-product-compliance
Lightning Source LLC
Chambersburg PA
CBHW030447290526
45786CB00001B/481